WINNING WAYS FOR LIFE
FINANCIAL & PERSONAL GROWTH

LIFE: TO LIVE, LEARN, LOVE, AND LEAVE A LEGACY

by MAUNG HLA WIN, CFP® *with*
ROBERT S. KEEBLER, CPA
EDWARD F. HOOPER, JD
KAY BIDWELL LOBERG

Cover design, Allen Win

Senior Editor, Kay Bidwell Loberg

Section Editor, Maria Kees

Prepared for printing by Allen Win

Book printing by

Publisher's ExpressPress
Ladysmith, Wisconsin 54848

Printed in the United States of America

By

Winning Ways for Life, LLC

www.WinningWaysforLifeLLC.com

ISBN 973-1-935920-09-0

Second Printing

To my wife, Rosemarie Win:
steadfast companion, source of joy,
my greatest cheerleader
and the sunshine on my shoulder.

M. Win

ACKNOWLEDGEMENTS

This book was truly a collaborative effort and I am grateful for the contributions of time, talent and suggestions from my co-authors: Foss, Robert and Kay.

I would also like to thank the following people for helping make the dream of producing this book a reality:

Kay Bidwell Loberg – for the many hours of discussion, writing, rewriting and editing; Maria Kees – especially for her assistance with Chapters 2, 4 & 7; Allen Win – for creating the book cover and formatting the book; Gary Roth – for his contribution to Chapter 7; Nathan Van Stippen – for his input on Chapter 2; Kim Petersen of the Community Foundation for the Fox Valley Region – for her contribution to Chapter 7; Keith Wilk; Laurie Scholl, Barb Slomski and The Staff of FISC; Bob Pedersen; Mike Vanevenhoven; Cindy Win; and my ever patient wife, Rosemarie Win.

I'd like to give special recognition to Foss Hooper and Dave Watters, who together were the catalyst that finally launched the book beyond the concept stage.

NOTE FROM MAUNG WIN, CFP®

This book, about growing personally while growing your financial wealth, is unique in many ways. The four active household words in the sub-title - To Live, Learn, Love, and Leave a Legacy - intertwine to play major roles in our lives. Life becomes more meaningful if one can identify how the concepts embodied in these beautiful words influence him or her. The more we recognize and live according to the message in each word, the better off we will be in life.

Life is a divine treasure. The essence of being alive is a gift and a blessing to us.

If we live well and do good deeds for others, learning from life experiences as we go, we enhance the probability of achieving success.

Learn new things, gain knowledge and skills. Knowledge is a powerful tool. Learning is a life long journey. Read, travel and explore a wide range of topics and activities to provide oneself a broad base of learning experiences.

As proclaimed in the Bible, love is patient and kind; love rejoices with truth. Love does not envy, is not pretentious, and will not be consumed in giving itself away. The more we love, the more our capacity for love grows. In my life, my faith and love for my children kept me alive during my darkest years. Love is everywhere and is revered in every religion. The Supreme Being loves us. The love for work is never labor, but gives joy and satisfaction.

Legacy is a powerful word with strong meaning. We want to be remembered by others: loved ones, family, children, grandchildren, and great grandchildren. A legacy can be embodied in material goods, good deeds, good will and philanthropic endeavors. The desire to leave a legacy is the force that propelled me to write this book.

Personal growth is an important aspect of the Winning Ways for Life. As a tree must add layers to its trunk and branch out to grow, people must grow in many directions to maximize their potential. And as healthy roots nurture the life force of a tree, so will a solid foundation in financial planning nurture your personal and financial growth. I have shared my journey. Now it is time for you to continue yours. Read the book. Follow the principles outlined here, and begin to reap the rewards that come from personal growth and financial well-being.

CONTENTS

FOREWORD

Do you want to be financially independent? Or, put another way, do you want to achieve personal financial freedom and family well-being? Only you can make that decision for yourself, and only you can make it happen.

From the time we are born, we encounter a variety of experiences and problems. No life is without its ups and downs. As others have said, it's not so much what happens to us, but how we respond, that will determine the outcome. Throughout our lives, we learn and live, live and learn. If one chooses not to learn from his or her life experiences, desired successes may never be achieved.

I would like to share with you my own roller coaster life experiences, filled with both failure and success. Faith, hope, love, perseverance, and determination played vital roles in overcoming my problems and achieving my successes. But what is success? For me, success is reaching that state of prosperity which allows for financial freedom, emotional stability, spiritual enrichment, family well-being and philanthropy. While this may sound unattainable to you now, often it is darkest before the dawn. Hopefully everyone will ultimately achieve his or her definition of success.

It took a great deal of courage for me to reveal my life story. Many unpleasant memories were buried for some years. Writing down the past has caused me to relive much of the pain and agony of my darker days. I went through many sleepless nights, nightmares, sweat and tears. I would have preferred to take an easier path.

I am not looking for sympathy for my failures, nor am I bragging of my successes. I managed to overcome the difficult times and took my success in stride. The fullness of my experience has made me a better, more complete person. Now, loving, cherishing, sharing with and caring for family as well as others have become the focus of my life.

Those who have heard my story encouraged me to share it with you so that you would understand why I believe the information in this book is so important and why I want to help others avoid some of my mistakes. My humble hope is that those who read about my life experiences may gain insight and inspiration for dealing with potential difficulties which may occur in their own lives. As such, this is my gift to you, the reader: sharing my story of dealing with the failures and successes of life.

I caution you not to take a word or words out of context. Read, interpret, and take positive action. My hope is that the younger people reading this will be able to avoid some of the mistakes I made.

M. Win

PART ONE

INTRODUCTION

This book was written to provide Maung Win, the primary author, with the opportunity to share his life experiences and learning with the reader in the hopes of inspiring insight into dealing with potential problems the reader may encounter. Win shares his vision that people are able to achieve a better quality of life, prosperity, spiritual enrichment and family wellbeing through financial literacy education. This book is also a life planning tool that can help individuals and families achieve their most desired goals.

To ensure the reader is getting the best information possible on the topics covered in this book, Maung Win tapped the expertise of Robert S. Keebler, CPA, MST, AEP, author of over 100 articles and columns, and editor, author or co-author of many books and treatises on wealth transfer and taxation; Edward F. (Foss) Hooper, J.D., an estate planning attorney dedicated to estate and wealth transfer planning, and co-author of books on philanthropy and estate planning; and Kay Bidwell Loberg, former credit counselor and financial educator with FISC, who has been a sounding board and editor for M. Win's articles and presentations for many years.

M. Win has been ably assisted in editing sections of the insurance, investment, and charitable giving chapters by Maria Kees, who completed a Bachelor of Science in Consumer Science and the CERTIFIED FINANCIAL PLANNER™ professional education program through University of Wisconsin-Madison. Gary Roth, CFP® with Watters Financial Group put together information for the charitable giving chapter, and Nathan Van Stippen, Financial Advisor, assisted with the investment chapter. Dave Watters, President and CEO of Watters Financial Group, has been instrumental in getting this book written and providing invaluable insight, contacts, and information.

Maung Win, CFP®, a volunteer for FISC, provides financial literacy education and planning services to the Fox Cities Community in Northeast Wisconsin. Though he has been able to touch the lives of many people, his impact has been limited by the fact that one person alone can counsel only so many individuals. We believe this book will allow him to reach out to many more people, within the community and beyond, with his message of help and hope.

Win provides pro bono services through FISC (the Financial Information and Service Center), the Small Business Administration program (SCORE), and the Financial Planning Association of NE Wisconsin. Pro bono simply means for the benefit of the community. In this case, volunteers provide financial education services to people in need of those services.

FISC, a private not-for-profit 501(c)3 organization, is a program of Goodwill Industries of North Central Wisconsin and a member of the National Foundation for Credit Counseling (NFCC). Goodwill Industries is under the leadership of Bob Pedersen, President and CEO, who offered support and encouragement for this project. Financial literacy is a main focus of the FISC mission. Proceeds from the sale of this book will be given to support financial literacy efforts and to provide resources for basic needs.

In addition to sharing Win's life story, the book addresses the following essential principles of complete financial and family well-being: fundamentals of financial planning, investment planning, retirement planning, insurance planning, IRA planning, estate planning, and charitable giving. These principles will be explained using real life illustrations whenever appropriate. In general, people tend to focus primarily on investment planning. To achieve true family wellbeing, it is necessary to incorporate all of the principles noted above.

In Maung Win's practice, he teaches and encourages his clients to follow these principles. Win attributes his own success to having personally followed the principles outlined in this book.

MAUNG WIN'S LIFE STORY

I was born, the youngest child and only son, in a family with three children in Moulamyine, Burma (now known as Myanmar), located in Southeast Asia. My father, U Taw Ba Thaung, was a prominent and successful attorney in our home town. My parents, devout Buddhists, sent me to a private parochial school to insure I had the best education available.

In 1953, at age 17, I graduated from St. Patrick's School and attended the University of Rangoon. In 1957, at age 20, I received two scholarships (Burmese military and Smidt-Mundt/Fulbright) to study medicine in the United States. Those scholarships and the opportunity they represented were one of my greatest achievements, and I felt like I was on top of the world.

As the only Burmese student at the University of Colorado in Boulder, I was lonely and homesick. There I met Kathy, my wife-to-be. We fell in love and got married, breaking the scholarship regulations. I lost both scholarships and was sent back to Myanmar in early 1959.

I had disgraced my parents, especially my father. A college degree and professional success were very important to him. I was also ashamed of my failure. There was a lot of gossip in my hometown community: the only son, spoiled by rich parents, had returned home as a failure. This failure was my greatest set-back in life so far. I had made some choices that came with negative consequences.

My parents welcomed Kathy warmly and graciously and treated her as their own daughter, though interracial marriage was uncommon at the time. Kathy is caucasian and was born in Rochester, N.Y. Since we arrived in Burma without jobs, my parents supported us and even bought us a house in Yangon.

Cynthia, the oldest of my three children, was born August 2, 1959 in Moulamyine, my own birth place. At that time, women usually gave birth at home with the help of a midwife. But Cynthia was born in a private hospital with all expenses covered by my parents. While we were grateful for their help, I was constantly reminded of my own short-comings in not being able to provide for my family on my own.

The failure of not having finished my education haunted me for almost three years, and I lived with shame, disgrace and disappointment. I wanted to prove, first to myself, and then to my father, that I could succeed in life. I needed a second chance to complete my education in America. I realized that my future in Burma, especially with a foreign wife, wasn't very promising. My daughter, being a Eurasian, or Burmese-American might also face obstacles to achieving a higher position in life.

Often I thought of returning to the U.S. to complete my education and start a new life in a land of many opportunities. But

Kathy had fallen in love with Myanmar, the Burmese people, culture and customs. Burmese people are wonderful people. Kathy wanted to stay in Burma. But in the fall of 1961, after many discussions regarding the pros and cons of living in Myanmar, we returned to America.

We arrived in the U.S. with less than $30 between us. Our plan was for me to attend college part time and work part time while Kathy worked full time. Kathy's parents, John Coleman and Dr. Babette Coleman, did not agree with our plan. They wanted both of us to attend college at their expense.

We attended the University of Rochester, where I studied chemical engineering and Kathy took Asian studies. We lived with my in-laws for one and one-half years. I was fortunate to have such cherishing and compassionate in-laws. Once again, we were dependent on others for our good fortune.

The difficulties of commuting to school, and day care issues with our daughter, made it important for us to find our own place. To pay for a small apartment and living expenses, Kathy worked part time at the University library Asian Center, and I worked part time at the University Medical Center as an orderly in the Emergency Room. My chores consisted of cleaning bedpans and undressing and washing the drunks who came in with knife or gunshot wounds. The weekends were horrible. I often found myself in the bathroom in tears.

I had never had a job like this and I struggled with inner frustrations. This was a drastic lifestyle change from state scholar status to cleaning bedpans. And it proved to be a significant life experience. I was living and learning.

Then we had David, our second child. Now there were four of us in a small off-campus one-bedroom apartment. Life got more complicated: family obligations, studying and part-time work. We struggled from paycheck to paycheck and couldn't afford to have anything like a week long vacation. We didn't take any kind of vacation for over four years, but were determined to persevere.

Upon graduation from the University of Rochester, I was hired by Colgate Palmolive Co. as a process engineer in Research and Development. While working at Colgate, I continued my studies and completed my master's degree in Management Science from Stevens Institute of Technology in Hoboken, NJ.

Allen, our third child, was born in Summit, NJ. Life was great now and everything seemed to be going well. However, the prosperity did not last long enough. Kathy and I grew in different directions and ended up separated in 1973. Although I had a very good job at Colgate, it was not enough to support my family and myself in separate households. My monthly paycheck was sent to my family for support and my own expenses were paid from borrowed money.

I rented a one-car garage that had been converted into a so-called "efficiency apartment". I called it a "dog house". It was furnished with a bed, a shower stall and a sink. There was no kitchen. The cooking facilities consisted of two small electric hotplates. Since there was no window for cross ventilation, the shower curtain was always covered with mildew. I lived in those damp, cramped and uncomfortable quarters for over six months.

I was ashamed that my friends might find out about my living accommodations, so I did not have a social life. And even if I had felt comfortable meeting with friends, I often found myself with only one dollar in my pocket. So there were no resources for entertainment of any kind. Only my two sons, David (10) and Allen (5), knew the condition of my place, since I had them on weekends.

Life became a continuous struggle for me. I had failed a second time. Life felt miserable, dehumanizing and depressing. I cried many nights. Often, I was so depressed that I wished I might not wake up the next morning. At the same time, I was fully aware that my children needed my love and financial support.

I was fortunate to have been exposed to Buddhism through my family's devotion, and to the Catholic faith due to attending a Catholic school when growing up. Believing in the power of faith and spiritualism helped me to overcome thoughts of ending my life. Wishing to die or attempting to take one's own life was not an answer, and I believe it is a grave sin. I did entertain the idea of joining a commune to escape my current existence, and even found one located in the backwoods of Pennsylvania. But this would have taken me further from my children, and I might be seen as having abandoned them. This, I could never do.

Special note to parents: Since I had my children with me only on weekends, special holidays and one full week during the year, I tried my very best to spend quality time with them. I never missed David's Police Athletic League football games. He played on both offense and defense because of his strong athletic capabilities. When he received the most dedicated player award on my 40th birthday, I wept with joy. That was one of my proudest moments. My encouragement to my children was, whatever the task may be, "do the best you can".

> *I wish I could have spent more time with them when they were growing up. I miss those years past. My message to parents who may be neglecting to spend time with their children: please start focusing on loving and cherishing them now. I salute those parents who treat love, affection, and care for their children as a top life priority. Time lost today will never be recovered.*

Much of my despair came from being broke and in debt. I got into debt, not because of exuberant living and irresponsible use of credit cards, but because I was trying to support two households on the same income that had been used to cover only one prior to the separation. There I was with a B.S. degree in Chemical Engineering and a Master's degree in Management Science and yet I lived in relative poverty.

Budgeting and cash flow management was less a problem than not having enough income to cover all expenses. It was scary to be so low on funds. I was concerned about having car trouble and being stranded because I couldn't afford to fix the car or have it towed to a safe location. At one point my car was almost repossessed due to late payments.

Often I prayed to Buddha and God to show me a path to get out of my situation. I would promise that, some day, if I were to achieve financial independence, I would volunteer my services to help bring financial education to others.

Life was horrible without money, or family to reach out to for moral support. The only family I had consisted of my three dependent children. Despite lack of resources, I could no longer stay in that one-room garage "apartment". I had to move out for my mental health, although I was aware that it was financially impractical. Ultimately, I was able to make the move to a one bedroom apartment. On the day I moved, my good friend, Richard Perry, came to help me. When he witnessed my living conditions, he was horrified and couldn't believe I had survived the "dog house".

As expected, living expenses went up. I needed a higher paying job to cover the higher cost of living. I left the Colgate Co. and joined International Playtex, Inc. Many challenges came with learning a different corporate culture and new product lines. But I learned to work smarter and harder, averaging 60 hours per week during the first two years.

My assignment was to modify the manufacturing process of household gloves to improve product quality. Once the assignment was successfully completed, I was promoted to the department manager position, all within two years of joining Playtex. The sweetest thing was that money came along with the promotion.

It seemed like my life might be stabilizing, but that was not to be the case. In 1975, the divorce case started, followed by five court hearings, including child custody, which I lost. In those days, the biological mother was usually awarded custody of the children. The financial toll from the divorce seemed astronomical at the time. My car was almost repossessed and my electricity was cut off for not paying the bills on time. I was $25,000 in debt. To be debt-free, I sold my share of the New Jersey house for $20,000 and paid off most of my debts. By 1981, I was debt-free, but without a house.

If I had been able to invest that $25,000 for a period of 30 years at an 8% annual interest rate return, the 2007 value of that investment would have been $250,000.

For six months, my mother had been seriously ill with cancer. I asked for an entry visa to Myanmar in order to spend some valuable time with my dying mother. The entry visa was denied by then-military dictator General Ne Win. There was no way to communicate with my mother, nor could I send any money for support. I could not express in words the pain and suffering from being denied the right to be with her. To date, I have not been able to come to complete closure on the death of my mother. It would seem that misery loved my company.

My message to you is to help and care for your loved ones while you can. Life is so short and we never know when the opportunity to be with them will be gone.

In spite of the misery, darkness and heartache that seemed to be my regular companions, there was sunshine on my shoulder when I met Rosemarie. Rosemarie was very kind, good and helpful to my two young boys, David (10) and Allen (5). She treated them like her own children. My daughter, Cynthia, was 15 then and more or less on her own, but there was a positive relationship between her and Rosemarie. Rosemarie was always there when I needed her, lifting my spirits during dark moments and sharing the joys that came our way.

My former father-in-law told me I would be stupid if I didn't marry Rosemarie. My former in-laws even attended our wedding, held on June 30, 1984. My middle child, David, was my best man, and Rosemarie's daughter, Mary Jo, was her maid of honor. We waited for ten years to make sure we had established a solid foundation and our relationship would be lasting. On June 30, 2009, Rosemarie and I celebrated our 25th wedding anniversary.

During my nine years at Playtex (1974-1983), I was unable to save for retirement due to a lack of surplus funds. Since I realized that I needed to start saving and build a fund for retirement, I was always in search of a better job with higher pay. In 1983, Bob Underhill, a Vice President at Kimberly Clark Corporation in Neenah, WI offered me a management position with a very good salary.

Upon leaving International Playtex, Inc., I received a lump sum of $50,000 from the profit sharing plan provided by the company. I should and would have rolled that lump sum into an IRA or the new company's 401(k) retirement fund. However, the advice I received from my accountant and an investment advisor was to collect the lump sum, take a 10% penalty, pay off the associated tax liability and then invest the balance.

The investment advisor put my money in an inappropriate investment vehicle that was not suitable for me. The investment went south and I lost all the money. I was not a well-informed investor and I was ashamed to admit my stupidity. The saying goes, "you'll see a light at the end of the tunnel". But in my case, I slammed into another wall. Again, I was living and learning, learning and living.

Once more, I promised myself that, one day, when I became financially independent, I would share my experiences to educate others. I really wanted to help people become informed investors and to inspire them to save toward retirement and family wellbeing. I was also accumulating experience in the "mistakes" department and believed I might be able to help others avoid them.

During my years at Kimberly Clark, I was contributing to college expenses for both of my sons. Since they didn't attend schools in the Wisconsin state system, we did not enjoy any reduced tuition benefits. But I was a proud father when each completed his college education. My daughter, Cynthia, did not attend college right after high school, but I tried to help her with expenses as much as I could. Later, she did graduate from college with honors, while continuing to hold down a job.

While helping my sons through school, I was able to bring my nephew, Thein Aye to the US to study at the University of WI, Oshkosh. He worked hard and paid his share of expenses toward attaining his degree. He returned to Burma, settled down with his own family, and is enjoying a good career with a Japanese firm in Yangon. To date, I continue to provide some financial support to my family in Myanmar.

Rosemarie was a school teacher in New Jersey. After we married, she continued to teach for an additional year in New Jersey. Then she took an early retirement option and joined me in Neenah in early 1985. We each put a down payment from our separate accounts into a marriage account; we didn't set up a pre-nuptial agreement. Family members from both sides have been treated equally and fairly.

I was very glad to have my wife attain the status of independent homemaker. She has earned the right to her retirement and deserves great respect. She has been my confidant as well as inspiration throughout the dark moments in my life. Without her, I would not be where I am today. Now I am able to see the "pot of gold at the end of the rainbow".

While the following results may not be "typical," the numbers are included to illustrate what is possible. I was fortunate to have achieved a high level of education and qualified for a very well-paying job. Not everyone will have access to the same income level. But everyone is capable of saving something and improving his or her situation through frugal living.

When I started to work for Kimberly Clark in 1983, my retirement 401(k) was a big "zero", although I had about $15,000 in an IRA account. I saved the maximum 19% of gross income in the 401(k) fund until I was given an early retirement option in 1995 at age 59. My 401(k) and IRA accounts grew to over $600,000. My wife's assets also reached over $400,000. The house was paid for with my severance pay, making us truly debt free (from rags to financial freedom!)

During my 12 years at Kimberly Clark, we carefully controlled our expenses, which included the mortgage, child support, college expenses and general living expenses. We were able to manage with one family income and still live comfortably.

Our road to financial and family wellbeing could be attributed to:

- Spending less than we earned and saving/investing the balance.

- Becoming informed investors.

- Investing prudently and for the long term.

- Living well within our means. (This is our motto and we strongly believe in the concept.)

In February of 1996, a few months after my retirement, I read an article in the Appleton Post-Crescent on "Grandma's Envelopes," written by Dennis Jansen, co-founder of FISC. It was an excellent article, but I noticed some of the cash flow calculations were incorrect, probably due to a misprint. I called FISC to congratulate them on the article and noted that the budget numbers presented were incongruent. A few days later, I received an invitation from John Robinson, the other FISC co-founder, to discuss some of FISC's programs.

I met Kay (then Aronowitz) Bidwell Loberg at the initial meeting. We discussed several topics regarding financial literacy education. The meeting was very productive and I accepted her offer to become a financial mentor to some FISC clients. This led to teaching a few financial education classes and to becoming a financial counselor for clients with investment-related questions or retirement concerns.

To provide better service to those in the Fox Valley of NE Wisconsin, a good friend and investment advisor, Kate Kessler, recommended that I register at the College for Financial Planning, Denver, CO in their CFP® Professional Education Program. The CFP® program is both comprehensive and challenging, consisting of five individual examinations and a ten hour comprehensive exam.

CERTIFIED FINANCIAL PLANNER™ or CFP® designation is the most prestigious honor in the field of financial planning. I followed Kate's recommendation, successfully completed the courses, and am proud to be a CFP® certificant. I have been a pro bono educator and Financial Planner at FISC from 1996 to the present, and orchestrated formation of a pro bono committee of the NE WI chapter of the Financial Planning Association.

During my service to FISC, I have been grateful to be able to touch the lives of many people from all income levels and age groups; teens to seniors. The objective is to help them improve the quality of their lives through the teaching and application of sound financial principles. The focus is on financial literacy education in basic money management, becoming an informed investor, preparing a sound financial plan and addressing a realistic retirement process.

The advice is objective since there is no commission on sales and no products or other financial services are involved. It has been a rewarding experience to have my dream of helping people in this way come true. Am I fully satisfied with the volunteer services I have been able to offer? Not quite. I often feel that I am a one-man crusade trying to reach out to everyone in the Fox Cities, where I reside. It's not enough. My desire is to expand my services beyond what one man can possibly achieve. I hope this book will be a vehicle to reach beyond our area and offer information and inspiration to those I may never actually meet.

PART TWO

THE COMPLETE PLAN FOR FAMILY FINANCIAL WELLNESS

The following fundamental principles are essential to building a successful plan for family financial well-being:

Wealth Management.

Knowing and applying the fundamentals of:

1. Financial planning

2. Investment planning, and

3. Retirement planning

4. Insurance planning via Risk Management.
   Having the appropriate type of insurance for:
   - Family protection
   - Family wealth transfer
   - Philanthropy

5. IRA Planning for Family Fortune:

   • Tax Advantage of Stretch IRA

6. Estate Planning

   • Effective arrangement of care for family members

   • Efficient transfer of wealth to beneficiaries or charity

7. Charitable Giving

Note that investment planning is only a portion of the entire financial wellness process. In general, some investment advisors tend to focus their clients directly on investment vehicles, and work to sell the client on a particular type of investment without learning the needs, goals and priorities of their client. In my practice, I advise my clients to follow all of the principles outlined above, as I follow them for my own financial wellness plan. It is important to me that I practice what I preach.

CHAPTER ONE

FUNDAMENTALS OF FINANCIAL PLANNING

Maung Win with Kay Bidwell Loberg

What is Financial Planning? First of all, financial planning is for everyone, no matter how much money an individual may or may not currently have. It is an ongoing process which helps one to effectively manage his or her money. The goal is to achieve personal and family financial wellness by controlling financial assets and liabilities to build net worth.

The Financial Planning Life Cycle© diagram on the following page is a learning tool that illustrates the lifelong planning process which can be used to achieve financial wellness goals. Practicing the steps provided will lead to benefits that reach far beyond the mere financial. Rewards include intangibles such as improved self-esteem, spiritual enrichment, and better quality of life, along with the tangibles of financial independence, an inheritable estate, and charitable contributions.

Where to begin? We'll walk through this process together, step by step, beginning with "Spend less than Income" and traveling counter-clockwise around the diagram.

Spend Less Than Income and Save the Difference.

This critical basic step must be accomplished in order to achieve financial goals. If you find your outgo exceeds your income, there are two possible options for bringing your budget into balance and finding money for saving. One option is to increase your income. While this may be challenging for many reasons, it is a viable option for a lot of people. And if not immediately attainable, an increased income is something to work toward by increasing education and marketable skills. The other option is to decrease spending. While many will initially see this as unrealistic, it may actually be the easier and more readily accomplished option.

Financial Planning Life Cycle

©2000 *Maung H. Win*
All Rights Reserved

Suggestions for trimming expenses include such simple items as making home-brewed coffee instead of grabbing the daily mocha latte at the local coffee house, and brown bagging lunch instead of hitting the fast food circuit. Once you calculate how much you've been spending on just these two items, the potential savings will probably surprise you. If you tend to eat out a lot in the evening, switching to more home-cooking can also reap significant savings. If eating out is important to you, consider looking for mid-week deals or going out for breakfast or lunch instead of dinner.

Drop the bells and whistles on your cable or satellite service and internet options. Pay for only the services you actually use, and consider giving up some services that you don't really need. Reduce your phone bill by using your cell phone for long distance and cutting out long distance on your land line, or completely eliminating your land line. Check out thrift stores, such as Goodwill, for great deals on clothing, books, toys and home decorations.

Evaluate your home, car, and health insurance to compare prices and look for cost savings. Comparison shop for all purchases. Use the internet to get savvy on costs of everything from books and slippers to appliances and cars.

Some people have found it helpful to "hide" extra money in their checking account in order to avoid overdrafts. They simply keep an extra $100 or so in the account that they don't include in their check register total. This is especially helpful if you have a habit of racking up overdraft fees. Just don't come to rely on using that cushion regularly, or you will likely spend it down and still overdraft your account.

Explore generic brands. They often cost significantly less than the name brand, but may offer similar quality or taste. Use coupons, but only if they are for products you would buy anyway. Make a list before you go shopping and stick to your list to reduce impulse purchases. Shop less frequently to avoid recreational spending.

While this list is by no means all-inclusive, implementing just a few of the above cost reduction strategies has helped many others to spend less than they make, and save the difference. Another great strategy for controlling spending is to ask yourself the following questions prior to making a purchase:

- Do I really need it, or just want it?

- How many hours do I have to work to buy the product I want?

- If I really need it, can I get a less expensive version? (i.e. seeing a car as a means of transportation rather than a status symbol, and buying a basic, reliable model rather than a luxury vehicle)

- Is this the best price/option for what I need? (Investigate providers and products for best deals.)

Many people have a "black hole" into which money seems to disappear without a trace. The way to find your black hole spending is to keep careful track of where your money is going. Carry a small notebook and record everything you spend, especially when paying cash. Be sure to record all check or check-card purchases and keep copies of all credit card transactions. It can be helpful to transfer your daily totals to a calendar for ease of tracking. Or use the Tracker form on the next page to help you find out where the money is going now.

Once a week, tally up your purchases to see how you have been allocating your money. Once a month, add up the weekly totals and review your receipts for spending patterns that may be draining you of valuable resources. Once you know where your money is going, you will be able to make different choices that will plug those black holes.

Tracker Month _____ **Year** _____

S	M	T	W	T	F	S

Totals:

The chart below illustrates the value of reducing spending, even on smaller items such as snacks, coffee, cigarettes or eating out for lunch. Choosing to save that $3, $5, or $7 a day instead of spending it, could lead to a nice savings account or emergency fund.

- $3 per day yields $1095 per year.

- $5 per day yields $1825 per year.

- $7 per day yields $2555 per year.

If the money is saved in an investment vehicle with an interest rate return of 6%, compounded annually, the following chart applies:

years	$1095/year	$1825/year	$2555/year
5	$6,175	$10,288	$14,403
10	14,433	24,055	33,677
15	25,487	42,479	59,470
20	40,280	67,133	93,987
30	86,569	144,281	201,994
40	169,464	282,440	395,417

The numbers above demonstrate the power of compounding interest; something known as the "time value of money". Albert Einstein said, "The most powerful force in the universe is compound interest."

Gather Data, Identify Current Status.

In order to get where you want to go, you have to know where you are now. The way to discover your current status is to gather as much information as possible on the personal and financial health of your immediate family. Having this data will provide you with valuable information for mapping out strategies and making decisions regarding your family's financial wellness plan.

The personal items to consider may include, but are not limited to:

- Size of family and ages of family members
- Family health information
- Anticipated longevity
- Spending habits/lifestyle expectations
- Risk tolerance
- Insurance
  - For protection
    - Disability
    - Life
    - Personal injury and property liability
    - Health
    - Home & auto
    - Long Term Care
  - As investment
    - Wealth transfer
    - Tax Management

- Estate information (for a legal opinion on completing these items, contact an estate planning attorney)
  - Will
  - Living Will
  - Durable Power of Attorney
  - Revocable Living Trust
  - Irrevocable Living Trust

The financial items to consider include, but are not limited to:

- Cash inflow/outflow
- Current investment information
- Retirement benefits
- Assets
- Liabilities
- Net Worth

Obtaining information on your current personal and financial status is a vital step in the planning process. Gathering the available pertinent data, and then dealing with any gaps, will help you achieve a sense of security regarding your financial future.

For example, being aware of the size of your family and the ages of its members will help you in planning for college education expenses and in obtaining appropriate levels of insurance in case of the premature death of the primary breadwinner or child care provider. Insurance is a protection planning instrument used to ensure adequate financial support through life's accidents, disasters and health threats.

You may not have been aware of the need for some of the listed estate planning documents. Now is the time to prepare any missing items. Dying without a will, or experiencing an incapacitating health issue without having a living will or durable power of attorney in place could leave your loved ones in a difficult situation. Your family could be left to make life and death decisions without knowing your preferences. Without a will, the state will make estate distribution decisions on your behalf without regard to what your wishes might have been.

Define, Prioritize, Establish Goals.

Spend some time to reflect on your goals – all of them. What do you hope to achieve in terms of education, material acquisition, professional success, travel experiences and retirement opportunities? Most of your goals will come with a price tag. Figuring out what you want to achieve will help to determine how much you will need to make it all happen.

You may want to live in a better neighborhood, purchase an upscale vehicle, attend a private college, buy a second home, get a boat, or vacation in Alaska or Hawaii. You may not have started a retirement fund, or you may not have thought about what you'd like to be able to do once you retire. Take all of these things into consideration as you begin to define your goals.

Once you have your goals identified, it is important to prioritize them. Differentiating between wants and needs will help to bring the list into focus. There will be some things that are very important to you, and others that may be nice to have, but not critical to your anticipated lifestyle or sense of well-being.

Making your goals as specific as possible will also help in determining both their cost and their value to you. Keep the goals realistic. Quantify the dollar amount needed to achieve each goal and the timeframe in which you'd like to have it achieved.

Goals related to financial well-being might look something like this:
- Have a written spending plan (by the end of the month)
- Effectively manage my money by spending less than I make (starting now!)
- Have an emergency fund of $500 (by the end of the year); increase the fund to $1000 (by June of next year)

- Buy a replacement vehicle (2 years)
- Have $10,000 for a home down payment (5 years)
- Pay off my student loans (3 years)
- Buy a $700 refrigerator (6 months)
- Complete a comprehensive financial plan (4 months)
- Pay off outstanding credit card debt (18 months)
- Plan for retirement

Evaluate/Analyze Budget.

To start constructing your personal spending plan, begin by estimating your income from all sources. Then estimate fixed and variable expenses. Subtract expenses from income to determine your excess or shortfall. Next consider your options for increasing savings and decreasing expenses to improve your bottom line.

Why is it important to establish an income and spending plan? A written plan can be used to control expenses, prevent or eliminate debt, enhance saving and investment, and ultimately help you achieve your financial goals. The real question then is, why would you not want to have such a plan? The spending plan is really the foundation for everything else that follows.

To help you get started, we've included a monthly expense worksheet with suggested spending categories. Filling in the major expenses may not be too difficult. You probably know how much you spend on utilities, cable, phone, rent or mortgage, car payment and student loans. You may not be so on top of more incidental spending, or even regular items that you just don't think about often.

Spending for groceries, gas, clothing and eating out might be harder numbers for you to pin down. The same tracking exercise that helps to plug "black hole" spending is very useful for getting a pretty good idea of spending in these more flexible spending categories. Write down everything you spend for a couple of weeks – a month is even better. Be honest about your purchases. And try to not let the tracking exercise influence your habits. At least not yet.

The idea is to get realistic numbers to complete the monthly expense worksheet. Once you feel you have a pretty good handle on where the money is going, you will be in a better position to evaluate current spending choices. When you get a good look at spending and compare it to income, you will know whether or not you are spending more than you make. If you are, you will probably have some credit card debt.

Monthly Expense Worksheet

CATEGORY	Monthly	Revised
Savings		
Housing		
Rent/Mortgage/Lot Rent		
2nd Mortgage/Home Equity		
Property Tax (not in mortgage)		
Heating		
Electricity		
Phone/Cell Phone/Pager		
Water/Sewage/Trash		
Home Maint/Improvement		
Furnishing/Appliances		
Lawn Care/Snow Removal		
Cleaning Supplies		
Groceries		
Food		
Paper Products		
Lunch/Snacks at work/school		
Pet Food		
Bulk Food Reserve		
Transportation		
Gas/Oil/Bus Fare		
Repairs & Maintenance		
Car Wash/Parking		
Licenses & Registration		
Car Lease/Payment/Replace		
Insurance		
Health Insurance		
Vehicle Insurance		
Homeowner/Rental Insurance		
Life/Disability Insurance		
Child Care		
Maintenance/Child support		
Child care/Day care		
Diaper expense		
Medical-Out-Of-Pocket		
Doctor		
Dentist/Braces		
Prescriptions		
Glasses/Eye Exams		
Chiropractic		
Counseling		
Name		
Date		

CATEGORY	Monthly	Revised
Clothing		
Clothing/Shoes/Boots		
Laundry		
Dry Cleaning		
Education		
School Supplies		
Tuition/Lessons		
Books/Papers/Magazines		
School pictures/Yearbook/etc		
Donations		
Church tithes/dues		
All Other		
Gifts		
Major Holidays		
Other Gifts		
Personal		
Professional Hair Care		
Personal Care Items		
Allowance/Petty Cash Adult		
Allowance(s) Child		
Cigarettes/Tobacco		
Alcoholic Beverages		
Entertainment		
Vacation/Weekend Trips		
Entertainment (dining/videos,Etc)		
Cable TV		
Babysitter		
Health/Social Clubs		
Gambling(Lottery/Casinos)		
Internet Access		
Miscellaneous		
Check/Money Order		
Union/Professional Dues		
Veterinary Care		
Hobbies		
Postage		
Tax Preparation		

Counselor Use Only	Current	Revised
Net Monthly Income		
Monthly Expenses		
Monthly Debt Payment		
Surplus/Deficit		

Credit cards allow us to spend beyond our means and avoid making spending decisions. At some point, either the payments get too large to handle, or the credit limit has been reached, and the spending choices get made for us. We no longer have the luxury of spending beyond our means. In fact, it may be necessary to really pull back on discretionary spending in order to pay off the debt and bring the budget back in balance.

Credit cards can be a great tool, if used properly. They can be a nightmare if abused. Once in the habit of charging and paying later, it's easy to build up a credit card balance that never goes away – especially if the cardholder makes only the minimum payment due each month. Those who pay only the minimum required amount often don't realize how much money they are wasting each month in interest fees. Add in a few late payments or over-limit fees and you are paying a hefty price for the privilege of using the credit card company's money.

Suppose you have a credit card with a $2000 balance and your goal is to stop using the card and pay it off in five years. Assuming an annual interest rate of 16%, your monthly payments would be $49. At the end of the five years, you will have paid $918 just in interest, which is 46% more than the original loan. Taking that $2000 loan from the credit card company cost you $918. Most people don't think of using their credit card as borrowing money, but that's exactly what is happening. You are borrowing money from the credit card company until you are ready to pay for the item you charged.

There are successful strategies for paying off credit cards. Some people start by paying off the lower balance cards first, making it easier for them to see progress and to most quickly reduce the number of cards in the debt picture. Others may prefer to start with the card charging the highest interest rate. This slows the overall growth rate of the debt more quickly. If you still aren't sure how to pay off the debt, there are professional credit counselors available to help turn the financial picture around. Just be sure to select an agency accredited by the NFCC, with certified counselors to help you, and you will receive the appropriate assistance for your situation.

You will keep more of your own money if you avoid building credit card balances and instead focus on paying yourself first. Out of each paycheck, set aside some money for future expenses, investing and retirement. The first priority here is to establish the easily accessed savings account, or emergency fund.

How important is an emergency fund? Very important. The fund will provide protection from unforeseen (or even likely) circumstances that can create financial stress for the unprepared. If you own a car, a computer, a refrigerator or a washing machine you know that things can break down, wear out and stop working at the most inopportune times. Your emergency fund will help you plan ahead for those events and put you and your car or appliances back in operation without having to sacrifice the utility or mortgage payments.

If you find it necessary to resort to credit to cover an emergency expense, you will likely have to pay 15% annual interest, or more, on that bill until it is paid off. If instead you have been able to set money aside in a savings account or money market fund, you will be receiving interest income of 2% or less. Admittedly, interest income is pretty low on the average savings account, but it's money coming in, not going out. And you will have the comfort of knowing the money is there when you need it.

In addition to your emergency expense fund, an ideal plan would have three to nine months of living expenses set aside in case of a job layoff, illness or other emergency. The easiest way to make sure you contribute to such a fund is to pay yourself first. This is also a good method for setting aside longer term savings. Designate a portion of your income for short and long term savings, and set up a plan to automatically transfer money from your paycheck into accounts specifically set up for your savings goals. Too often, if this payment is put on the back end of the expenses, all the money is spent before anyone thinks about saving.

Financial Position Statement.

A statement showing your current assets and liabilities gives you a snap shot of your current financial position. It is the best indicator of your actual personal wealth or net worth. A person may make a lot of money and may have a large, well-decorated home, along with an expensive vehicle. But that same individual . may also be carrying a lot of debt; which means his or her net worth would probably be relatively low.

The formula for determining net worth involves subtracting your liabilities from your assets. The road map to a winning financial future includes turning liabilities into assets to increase net worth. Minimizing or eliminating debt will improve net worth. Increasing your assets will also improve net worth. Sound investment in appropriate investment vehicles is a way to increase assets.

There are many types of investment vehicles, some more common than others. The list below offers the range of investment options available.

- Savings accounts
- Money Market funds
- CDs
- Stocks (ownership in a specific company)
- Mutual funds (general ownership in a diversified portfolio)
- Bonds (debt securities, lending money)
- Real Estate
    - Personal Home
    - Rental Property
    - REIT (Real Estate Investment Trust)
- Coins/Precious Metals
- Annuities
- Insurance

We will go into more detail on investment options later, but for now, know that there are many from which to choose. The earlier exercises of gathering data on your current financial status, establishing and prioritizing goals, and evaluating your budget and financial position will be used to determine which investment vehicles might best suit your goals, temperament, and risk tolerance.

The following page provides an example of a completed financial position statement. Use the example to help you fill in your own statement and determine your current net worth. Remember, net worth is a good indicator of your current financial health. To improve financial wellness, it will be necessary to increase assets and/or decrease liabilities.

JACK & JILL HAPPY (family of 5)
Statement of Financial Position

ASSETS[1] (What you own)

A. Cash/Cash Equivalents

Checking account	$	6,000*
Credit union savings account		9,000
Money market account		15,000
Life Insurance Cash Value		19,500
Total Cash/Cash Equivalents	**$**	**49,500**

B. Invested Assets

Stock portfolio	$	9,000
Mutual Fund portfolio		21,000
401 K		90,000
IRA(s)		24,000
Vested portion of Pension		18,000
Total Invested Assets	**$**	**162,000**

C. Use Assets

Residence	$ 330,000
Autos	60,000
Personal property	120,000
Total Use Assets	**$ 510,000**

TOTAL ASSETS: A+B+C = $721,500

LIABILITIES & NET WORTH (What you owe)

Liabilities[2]

Credit card balance	$ 1,500
Auto note balance	10,500
Mortgage note balance	215,400
Total Liabilities	**$ 227,400**

ASSETS LESS LIABILITIES = NET WORTH
$721,500 – 227,400 = $494,100

1 Presented at FAIR MARKET VALUE
2 Principal Only
* Emergency Fund

Recommend/Implement Action Plan.

Now that you know where you are and where you want to go, you are ready to implement an action plan that will move you toward your financial goals. The Action Plan is a starting point, not an ending. And the Plan is a living document in the sense that it will need to be revisited and revised throughout your life. As your circumstances change - marriage, children, children grow up, divorce, retirement - it will be necessary to adjust your plan to reflect your new realities.

The best plan in the world is no good unless it is implemented. As illustrated on the Financial Planning Life Cycle diagram, this is a continuous process that requires your active participation. Once you have decided on your plan of action, it's time to act!

CHAPTER TWO
INVESTMENT PLANNING

Maung Win with Nathan Van Stippen, Maria Kees
& Kay Bidwell Loberg

Many published financial books have focused primarily on investments and investing. As mentioned in previous chapters, investing / investment return is only a part of comprehensive financial planning. The intent of this chapter is to educate the reader to an understanding of important concepts, terminology and considerations necessary to becoming an informed investor. To achieve this we will discuss various types of investment products, concepts, principals and strategies. However, we will not be suggesting purchase of specific investment products: our objective is to offer information.

The key to sound investing is to have a clear understanding of your goals and objectives. Goals and objectives should be realistic, attainable and quantifiable in a dollar amount tied to a given time frame. Generally, a person invests for some specific future benefit such as buying a home, getting a college education, or retirement. That "future benefit" is the goal. The objectives are the steps taken to achieve that goal. The list of possible goals is as varied as individual wants, needs and desires.

Investment Strategy

The foundational principals for sound investing begin with the investor researching and understanding each option before investing. Invest in something you know, read the prospectus, know and understand your risk tolerance – avoid complex strategies you don't understand. Diversify by allocating your funds among different economic sectors. Margin accounts, futures and options are multifaceted investment strategies that should be avoided by beginners, as well as attempting to time the market or taking out equity loans for investment capital.

Short term investments should be used for specific purposes (i.e. to purchase a car or put a down-payment on a home) with consideration for risk tolerance. In general, invest for the long term and do not let your emotions dictate your investment decisions. Create an investment policy and strategy to avoid emotional moves in and out of investments. Investment objectives should be clearly defined and be consistent with your risk tolerance. For example, mutual funds have stated objectives such as growth, income, balanced, or international. Funds also have various levels of risk – very aggressive to very conservative. It is important to match your investments with your personal goals and risk tolerance.

Although there have been periods of significant volatility in the stock market, historically, the market has recovered from its downturns. Over the past 60 years there have been twelve Bear Markets (two consecutive quarters of market downturn) lasting an average of fourteen months, with an average decline of 23.7%. During those same 60 years, there have been twelve Bull Markets (market upturns) lasting an average of 45 months, with an average incline of 157%.

To summarize, have an investment strategy, don't let your emotions rule your decisions, don't try to time the market, invest for the long term and reposition your portfolio whenever appropriate. An investment strategy considers the following as a template that you, as an investor, can build upon: the time value of money, proper diversification and asset allocation, risk management, tax implications and types of investments. The following information will help clarify each component of this template.

Time Value of Money

The earlier one begins to invest, the longer the time horizon for realizing one's investment goals. The magic of compounding interest will work in your favor as interest accrues, your balance grows, and the amount now used to factor gains has added value to your account.

Diversification and Asset Allocation

Many investors view diversification and asset allocation as the same concept, but they are very different. The rationale for each might seem similar, but diversification and asset allocation function to achieve their own specific purposes.

Diversification is investing in various stocks or other investments over a broad spectrum of asset classes to reduce investment risks through safety in numbers. Investing all your money into one stock is very risky; thus owning multiple stocks among different asset classes will offset the risk of poor performance or failure of one or a few stock holdings. As a well diversified investor, spreading your assets around to cover multiple asset classes will allow you to limit significant losses or capture gains when only a portion of the market is affected.

Asset allocation differs from diversification in that you are allocating resources over multiple investment types. Specifically, this means having your investments not only in multiple stocks, mutual funds and ETFs (exchange traded funds), but utilizing annuities, bonds, options, CDs (certificates of deposit), cash, real estate, foreign currencies, and commodities, among other possibilities.

The reason asset allocation carries such importance is that performance of individual asset categories can vary tremendously from year to year. If you are invested in only one asset category, you might see your assets declining while other investment types are realizing gains. A well allocated investment portfolio can counteract and smooth out the performance of the investments if one asset category is negatively affected. Therefore it is very important to review your investments and reposition your portfolio whenever appropriate.

Risk Management

Risk is the uncertainty that the anticipated return on an investment may or may not be achieved. Before one can assess his/her risk tolerance, it is important to know various "risk" involved with investment planning. The following list will give an idea of risks that should be taken into consideration.

- *Marketability risk:* the ability to buy or sell an asset quickly and easily (e.g. actively traded stocks).
- *Liquidity risk:* the chance that it will not be possible to quickly convert an investment to cash (i.e. real estate investment).
- *Purchasing Power risk:* relating to inflation or deflation within the economy (i.e. investments that have low returns, such as savings accounts, are not likely to keep up with inflation).

- *Interest Rate risk:* caused by fluctuations in the general level of interest rates (if interest rates increase, prices of bonds and stock prices decrease, and vice versa).
- *Market risk:* circumstances that affect investment returns in the overall level of the stock market (factors include political climate, inflation expectations, higher interest rates, unemployment conditions).
- *Reinvestment rate risk:* a chance that there will not be an opportunity to reinvest coupon payments and principal at maturity at an acceptable rate.
- *Financial risk:* associated with the mix of debt and equity used to finance a firm (the greater the leverage, the greater the risk).
- *Default risk:* the risk that the firm cannot meet its debt obligation.
- *Business risk:* risk associated with a specific industry or firm. A negative effect on the value of a firm, but not affecting the whole market.
- *Exchange rate risk:* risk associated with changes in the value of foreign currencies.
- *Country risk:* risk associated with the politics of the country where the business is located.

There are a few different methods of investing that can help alleviate some of the risk burden and smooth out dramatic increases and decreases in your investment portfolio. Dollar cost averaging and dividend reinvestment are two strategies that can be used to achieve less volatile results.

Making monthly or weekly contributions through a 401(k) or Roth IRA is a common example of dollar cost averaging. Investing smaller amounts at regular intervals gives the investor an invested amount that is the "average" of all purchases made over a specified period of time. This method helps the investor avoid having to time the market and risk investing a large sum at a market peak.

Dividend reinvestment is another method of dollar cost averaging. Instead of cashing dividend checks, reinvest them in your portfolio. This will increase the number of shares owned, and over time, increase the likelihood of investment growth.

The risk/return trade-off is a fundamental investment planning concept. Often, a high rate of return is associated with a high level of risk. Invested assets will fluctuate over time, so it is important to stay true to your investment plan. Evaluate your ability to tolerate risk and investment fluctuations, and choose investments that fit your goals, time horizon, and risk tolerance.

Tax Considerations

An important consideration while creating your investment plan is potential tax implications. Taxes can have a dramatic impact on an investment strategy; proper tax planning creates the ability to focus on wealth maximization, not just tax savings. Do not pass up good investments in order to save on taxes alone, but do evaluate each investment strategy to be sure it works in conjunction with your individual tax situation.

It is important to know the difference between tax free and tax deferred. In a tax free investment, there are no taxes on income or withdrawals. Examples include tax-exempt municipal bonds or Roth IRAs. Tax deferred simply means that taxes are only due upon withdrawal of the funds, such as from a deferred annuity, income annuity, 401(k), 403 (b) or traditional IRA.

Be careful to understand the difference between tax avoidance – planning within the law to minimize tax liability, and tax evasion –

fraud or other illegal means to reduce or eliminate tax liability. The latter can result in fines or even imprisonment. Always be sure your taxes are filed on time to avoid costly penalties.

Types of Investments

There are numerous types of investments available, and it is important to have a basic understanding of each of these investment classes before deciding in what to invest. There are cash equivalents, stocks (ownership in a company), mutual funds & exchange traded funds (general ownership in a diversified portfolio), bonds, annuities, real estate, precious metals and other commodities.

Money Market Account

Money Market Accounts are considered cash accounts. A Money Market account generally works similarly to a checking account, and provides the easiest access to the invested funds. Money Market accounts usually require minimum investments and the interest rate offered on a Money Market account is often linked to the amount invested. The more money you keep in your account, the higher the potential return on investment. This is considered a low-risk investment, and the interest rates reflect that reality. However, a Money Market account is not FDIC insured.

Certificates of Deposit

Certificates of Deposit (CDs) are invested at a given rate for a specified period of time. Generally, the longer the money is invested, the higher the interest rate; and the larger the amount invested, the higher the interest rate offered. CDs are FDIC insured. However, you will not be able to access your money until the end of the investment period without incurring a penalty for early withdrawal.

Stocks

A purchase of stock involves buying a share or shares in a given company. For those with only limited dollars to invest, it is not recommended to buy individual stocks, because this will not allow for easy diversification of funds. If all of your investment dollars are with one company, and that company falters, the negative impact will be much greater than if you had your resources spread among several companies.

For those with greater resources to invest, individual stocks may represent a very suitable investment choice. Again, much depends on the goals and objectives of the individual investor.

Since stocks represent an investment which intrigues a large number of investors, and there is much to know about investing in stocks, a more in-depth look at analyzing stock selection is shared later in this chapter.

Mutual Funds, Exchange Traded Funds and Hedge funds

Mutual funds receive investment dollars from investors seeking professional money management and a diversified portfolio. A mutual fund manager pools the investors' money to purchase various securities – stocks, bonds, treasury bills, notes, etc. This offers investors with limited resources the opportunity to achieve greater diversification and meet their investment goals with a well allocated portfolio.

There are basically four categories of mutual funds: income, growth, balanced, and convertible securities. With so many funds available, and each having its own objectives, it is important to select the appropriate type of funds to meet your individual objectives.

When researching mutual fund options, it is important to note fees and expenses of the various share classes as well as return on investment. Share class fees range within each particular share class from up front sales charges (front load), to contingent deferred sales charges, no load, and exit fees.

An Exchange Traded Fund (ETF) is an investment fund traded on stock exchanges, much like stocks. Most ETFs are designed to follow a specific index (such as the S&P 500) or sector of the market. ETFs may be attractive investments because of their low costs, tax efficiency, and stock-like features.

A hedge fund is another type of investment vehicle. Hedge funds are similar to mutual funds in that they consist of pooled funds from various investors and are professionally managed. However, hedge fund investors consist of a limited number of sophisticated investors with high net worth and very high income, capable of making large investments.

Hedge funds use high risk, aggressive strategies, such as short selling, leveraging, and derivative investing. Though hedge funds can be used to offset, or hedge against, the risk of other assets, the strategies used in many hedge funds today are designed to maximize returns and are often more volatile than the market. Hedge fund investing is not recommended for average investors.

Annuities – Fixed, Indexed, and Variable

A vast number of complex investment options are available today; annuities are a prime example of this. An annuity is an insurance product which can insure retirement savings to varying degrees. We'll discuss the three primary types of annuities: fixed, indexed, and variable annuities.

While initially resistant to annuity products, Win now has 24% of his investment portfolio in annuities. Each of these annuities is used in conjunction with a death benefit.

Fixed annuities are fairly straightforward – the investor gets a certain rate of return. The interest rate may be guaranteed for a set number of years, or may fluctuate with a guaranteed minimum rate. The interest earned is tax deferred until it is withdrawn, and various rules allow for penalty-free withdrawals during the surrender charge period. Pay attention to the annuity contract's surrender charge period. The duration dictates the length of the surrender charge period, with the surrender percentage amount typically decreasing over the duration of the contract. For instance, a fixed annuity product may offer a guaranteed interest rate of 5.00% for 6 years, with a surrender charge that starts at 6%, and decreases by 1% after each annual anniversary.

Indexed, fixed indexed, or equity indexed annuities are all the same product by different names. These types of annuities can, but may not always have a declared minimum rate of interest while providing limited exposure to the market. They offer the opportunity for higher rates of return while eliminating any downside risk during times of market downturn. Contracts are most often linked to a market index like the Dow Jones Industrial Average or the S&P 500, and provide a portion of the gain in the market index. Again, be careful, these contracts can be very costly if withdrawn during the surrender charge period.

Finally, there is the variable annuity. Variable annuities can be valuable as an investment planning tool and typically offer guarantees, such as an income benefit or a death benefit, or both. The guarantee amounts are different from the investment's value. Variable annuities are very useful tools, but can be damaging if you are not aware of the costs involved and if the product with its riders and benefits does not fit your needs. Make sure the benefits are appropriate for the goals and needs of the investor.

Annuities have carried a negative connotation for years, sometimes with good reason. While there are very good annuity products available, some annuity products are sold in situations where they are not appropriate for the investor. Annuity and life insurance products are perceived as poisonous to many investors as a result of misrepresentations by some deceitful sales persons. Good annuity and life insurance products, when properly presented and implemented, can be excellent products for retirement investment.

In order to understand and invest in an annuity that is appropriate for your investment plan, it would be prudent to consult with an ethical, knowledgeable advisor. Read investment-related journals and the prospectus for any investments you may be considering to help avoid unsuitable investments.

Approach & Analysis for Stock Selection

Two basic approaches to stock analysis are fundamental analysis and technical analysis. Fundamental analysis of a stock emphasizes the belief that a company's strength, such as growth and earnings, will dictate the underlying stock price. This type of analysis helps in identifying overvalued and undervalued securities. Fundamental analysis includes evaluation of some of the following areas:

- *The Economy* - The economic environment takes into consideration phases of the business cycle, the Federal Reserve monetary policy (as determined by Ben Bernanke and the regional Federal Governors), and gross domestic product (GDP). These factors can influence corporations as well as consumers.

- *Type of Industry* - (Cyclical, Defensive/Stable, and Growth) Changes in the economic environment can have a major impact on various industries. During a period of inflation and high interest rates, cyclical industries don't fair very well. Most cyclical industries manufacture durable goods such as heavy equipment, steel, automobiles, appliances and buildings. Defensive/stable industries are least affected by the above economic conditions. These defensive industries produce food, pharmaceuticals, and non-durable consumer products such as personal and family products.

  During a period of healthy economic growth, industries such as biotechnology and computer makers do well. The productivity, profitability and earnings in these industries grow faster than many other industries.

- *Individual Companies* - This third component of fundamental analysis is the company itself. The key features are financial strength, management philosophy, productivity, profitability and earnings.

Technical analysis utilizes charts and graphs of past stock price movements and trading volume to determine future price movements. Timing of buying and selling is a primary emphasis of this type of analysis, rather than a company's fundamentals.

In addition to fundamental and technical analysis, the following factors may be considerations in stock evaluation:

P/E ratio is the ratio of the price of the stock to the earnings per share of that stock. Generally, stocks with low P/E ratios are more conservative than stocks with high P/E ratios. Companies with steady and stable earnings have lower P/E ratios, while companies with high earnings growth have higher P/E ratios.

Price to sales ratio is the ratio of market value (current stock price x number of shares outstanding) to annual sales (this information is available from the company's annual report.) Generally, stocks with a low price-to-sales ratio are believed to be more conservative than stocks with a high price-to-sales ratio.

Price to book value is defined as the stock price divided by the asset value of a stock. Firms having low price-to-book ratios are expected to be more conservative than those with high price-to-book ratios.

β coefficient is an index (number) of the volatility of an individual stock relative to the volatility of the market. The higher the *β* the greater the volatility of the stock. This measure can help you determine the price volatility of a stock.

Value Line phenomenon describes the situation where those stocks ranked "1" in timeliness by the *Value Line Investment Survey* are supposed to perform better than those rated "5" by the survey. A "1" rating is the best and "5" the worst. *Value Line* is available at most local libraries.

Choosing an Investment Advisor

The first step of your investment journey is to determine why you are investing; and next, how you plan to invest. The "why" seems pretty simple to answer… "to grow my money in the market." But there is more to consider. Are you investing long term or short term? Is it for retirement or for the purchase of a home, car or education? How much risk are you willing to take? What will you invest into? The questions go on and on. But how do you answer all of these questions? Many investors don't take the time to figure out "why." Others decide to have someone else help answer the questions. But who can really help and can you trust them to have your best interest at heart?

Trying to identify those who can provide you with good advice is no easy task. Extensive interviews with multiple professionals in multiple professions may have to be conducted. It is helpful to identify a group or team of independent advisors with expertise in various areas of specialty who work with other professionals such as accountants (CPAs), estate planning attorneys and even other financial advisors.

This process often starts with asking other successful individuals who they worked with and what their results have been. Ask for a resume from recommended advisors days before setting up an interview. This can help you refine your pool of potential advisors based on experience, education, levels of success and activities. Since it is difficult to find one person able to be an expert in all areas of financial planning and investing, it would be prudent to seek a professional who is willing to collaborate with other experts. A group or team of experts to break down, assess and analyze your individual situation will be in a better position to provide you with in-depth reports and multifaceted solutions for any areas of concern. Your chosen team should help you to identify and establish your goals for retirement, wealth preservation, tax avoidance and wealth transfer.

To ensure the most well-rounded approach to your investment planning, it would be wise to consider independent advisors working with a group of other experts. Independent advisory groups can get unbiased information from the entire spectrum of investment options instead of being limited to a specific product line. While captive advisers may be able to offer limited investment options to clients, some independent advisors have the ability to employ non-traditional investment products for maximum allocation and diversification exposure.

Also note that some investment advisors are known to "churn" investments – constantly calling investors with recommendations to buy and sell in order to make a commission. Conversely, some advisors forget about the investor once a purchase is made, and you rarely hear from them. It is not unusual for an advisor to steer clients to certain investments solely for profitability of his/her company, because the advisor is required to meet certain revenue quotas or is trying to hit bonus goals. Remember, the advisor is in this to make a living and may favor products which improve his or her own bottom line. At the same time, those products may also be excellent investments for the client.

The key here is objective, independent goal-based planning. Have a properly defined plan for your goals, both long and short term - for retirement income and estate management (discussed in other chapters), as well as gifting to children and charities. In-depth risk tolerance profiles offer options for investing into investment vehicles that will help to achieve desired goals. Find a financial planner/advisor who is ethical, places the client first, and selects appropriate products and services that are consistent with your risk tolerance, goals, needs and priorities.

Upon leaving International Playtex, Inc., in 1983, I received a lump sum of $50,000 from the profit sharing plan provided by the company. I should and would have rolled that lump sum into an IRA or the new company's 401(k) retirement fund. However, the advice received from an accountant and an investment advisor was to collect the lump sum, take a 10% penalty, pay off the associated tax liability and then invest the balance.

I asked the investment advisor to invest my money in a growth fund to be used for retirement. However, the advisor put the money in a high risk tax advantaged real estate partnership product without providing a good explanation for the investment.

This investment was inappropriate for me and did not meet my objective and goal. The investment went south and I lost all the money. I was not a well-informed investor then, and was ashamed to admit my ignorance. This was a real learning experience, and one of the few investment pitfalls I encountered.

The lesson I learned is that even if you are using professional advisors, you need to understand your investments and the associated risks.

Establishing goals and placing the investments is only the beginning of your process for the investment plan. After implementation of the investment plan, the plan must be monitored to be sure it remains in line with the goal(s) of your strategy. Periodic evaluation of the investments is necessary to identify any changes that may be required to meet your financial objectives.

CHAPTER THREE
RETIREMENT PLANNING

Maung Win

What is retirement planning?

Retirement planning is a lifelong process. It parallels the financial planning process discussed in the Fundamentals of Financial Planning. Whether you are in your 20's or over 50, planning, executing and implementing the retirement plan are essential to reaching your retirement goals.

In retirement, everyone would like to be financially independent, financially worry-free, and in a position to enjoy life. This is often referred to as achieving the American Dream for retirement. To get there, it will be important to:

- Manage cash flow effectively (spend less than you make and save/invest the balance.)
- Accumulate assets
- Minimize liabilities
- Build net worth.

Ultimately, you will be looking to preserve your wealth, which will allow you to live comfortably in retirement and provide opportunities for wealth distribution. Managing your finances well will provide you the legacy of having assets to distribute among designated beneficiaries, including family members and charities, as you see fit.

While the goal of both financial and retirement planning is to achieve personal and family financial wellness now and in the retirement years, each individual will define that "wellness" differently depending on his or her needs and wants. And for many, there will be intermediate goals that must be met to insure the success of the retirement plan. Some general goals that may apply to your current situation include:

- Learning to live within a budget
- Paying off a mortgage
- Minimizing or eliminating consumer debt
- Maximizing savings/investments to build a substantial retirement nest egg
- Setting aside extra dollars to defray the cost of medical and dental expenses. Even those who receive company health care credits might discover the credits are not enough to cover all expenses.

Recognizing hurdles in achieving desired retirement dreams:

Many people are unaware of all the issues to consider when putting together a retirement plan. Others are simply not ready for retirement because they have not planned at all, or their plans were inadequate.

Some individuals set goals that are too ambitious or unrealistic, and others begin saving too late. Many pre-retirees choose a lifestyle which is beyond their means, leaving nothing for saving or investing before retirement. Or, once retired, those who did save live beyond their means and deplete their resources too rapidly.

Sometimes the problem in reaching the desired goal is in the choice of investments used to fund a retirement plan (refer to Investment Planning chapter). Investments which are too conservative may not grow enough to provide adequate resources. Investments which are too aggressive run the risk of losing principal in an economic downturn. Inefficient investment portfolio management can make growth of investments slower than necessary, creating the potential for outliving one's retirement savings.

Consider investing in a target date retirement fund during your working years. After retirement, revert to more moderate/conservative investments. The key is to have balanced income and growth fund strategies to accumulate as well as preserve wealth while approaching retirement and during retirement years.

Target Retirement Funds				
Target Date	2012	2017	2025	2025-2050
Risk Level	Conservative	Moderate	Moderate to Aggressive	Very Aggressive
Cash/Stable Value	42%	24%	5%	0%
Diversified Bond Funds	30%	38%	14%	10%
Large Cap US Stocks	13%	17%	32%	34%
Mid & Small Cap US Stocks	8%	11%	27%	30%
Foreign Stocks	7%	10%	22%	26%

Chart is for illustration purposes only. Actual percentages may vary.

Not understanding, or ignoring, the power of inflation can also cause one to make poor investment choices. Investments that do not keep up with inflation will result in a loss of buying power.

To overcome the obstacles to achieving the American Dream of retirement, we offer the following suggestions:

- Begin effective management of your monthly budget (if you do not already have a good spending plan in place) as described in the chapter on Fundamentals of Financial Planning.
- Do not depend on your employer to provide a company pension. Most companies no longer offer this benefit.
- Consider Social Security income as only a supplement to your other resources.
- Take charge of your retirement and assume an active role in establishing your own retirement accounts.
- Take advantage of plans offered through employers, or those for self-employed individuals, such as 401(k), 403(b), 457 plans, SEP, Simple, Keough, etc.
- Contribute to Roth and/or traditional IRAs as allowed.
- Set aside additional non-qualified investment funds once the limits of qualified investments are reached.

Securing your future pot of gold

The "Future Pot of Gold" diagram on the following page illustrates the importance of incorporating every possible option listed above to ensure a stable retirement. In the past, many people relied on the traditional three-legged stool to provide a secure retirement. Combining Social Security with a company pension and personal savings allowed many to retire comfortably and achieve their desired retirement dreams.

Today, with company pensions generally a thing of the past and restrictions placed on qualified contributions, a four-legged stool is recommended for greater stability. In addition to Social Security and workplace-related retirement plans, the IRAs and personal savings allow for maximizing investment dollars. The four-legged stool provides greater security for retirement dollars, assuming a variety of investment vehicles and funds are used.

Future Pot of Gold

Traditional (3-Legged Stool)
- Social Security
- Company Pension
- Personal Savings/Investments
  Real Estate

Today (4-Legged Stool for Stability)
- Social Security
- Personal Savings/Investments
  Real Estate
- IRAs (Traditional & Roth)
- Retirement Plans
  401k, 403b, etc.

Employer-sponsored plans

At any time, but especially in times of economic uncertainty, long-term participation in employer-sponsored retirement plans, such as a 401(k), 403(b), or other retirement plan is essential. Short-term economic gyrations have no profound effect on long-term investment results. While past performance is not necessarily indicative of future results, historically, long-term investments have performed very well.

Retirement plan participants may be classified into three groups: (1) those who fully maximize participation, (2) those who only partially participate, and (3) those who do not participate/enroll. To improve the likelihood of retiring comfortably with a healthy retirement fund, it is important to participate and take advantage of company sponsored plans. At the request of some employers, Win has participated in educating groups of employees about their company sponsored retirement plans and the benefits of enrolling. The outcomes have been very rewarding for both employees and employers.

There are several great reasons for investing in a company sponsored retirement plan:

- Many employers match all or a portion of the employee's contribution, up to 6% of gross salary (It's like getting free money!)
- This is a pretax investment which reduces your tax liability for the year in which the contribution is made. (Maximum contribution in 2010 is $16,500, with a catch-up option of an additional $5500 for those over 50.)
- The taxes are deferred until a qualified withdrawal is made.
- There is opportunity for diversification within the plan.

- These long-term investments take advantage of the time value of money as it relates to the power of compounding interest.

- Regular contributions bring about the benefits of dollar cost averaging.

- Long-term investment results are less affected by periodic economic downturns.

- These funds are protected from creditors.

Social Security income alone is inadequate for most people. It was never intended to be the sole source of retirement income and will cover only very basic living expenses. To give yourself the greater financial freedom that comes from having a bigger retirement pot, consider fully maximizing contributions to your company plan.

As mentioned in the section on "Win's Life Story", my experience with the 401(k) plan is proof of the impact that employer sponsored retirement plans can have on retirement planning. Beginning with my working years with Kimberly-Clark, I contributed the maximum allowable amount to the company's 401(k) plan and my employer matched 50% of my contribution (up to 6% of salary). On top of that, I was able to put an additional 10% of my salary into my 401(k)plan. My commitment to maximizing my 401(k) contribution allowed me to retire early, at age 59.

Traditional IRA & Roth IRA

For even greater financial independence and enjoyment in your golden years, consider an Individual Retirement Account (IRA). Traditional and Roth IRAs are investment vehicles that were created for those with earned income to be able to set aside a portion of their earnings in a qualified plan. The IRA information provided in this chapter offers a brief overview of the IRA as an investment vehicle. Robert Keebler's chapter on IRA Planning will further explain IRAs as a tax-advantaged investment tool.

To fund an IRA, you must have earned income or be receiving alimony. There are income limits for participation eligibility in both traditional and Roth IRAs, and contribution limits depending on income. IRA contributions cannot exceed the lesser of a) the allowable contribution, or, b) the taxpayer's compensation included in gross income. For 2010, the allowable contribution is $5000, unless the account holder is over 50. Those over 50 are allowed to contribute an additional $1000 as part of a "catch-up provision". Check on-line resources such as: http://www.irs.gov/publications/p590/index.html for current income and contribution limits.

IRA funds may be invested in a broad range of investment vehicles with some exceptions. Life insurance contracts and collectibles are not allowed. Qualified investments include the American Eagle gold coin, and platinum or palladium bullion. Funds may not be used to provide loans to disqualified persons or for collateral purposes.

In a traditional IRA, the maximum age for making contributions is $70^1/_2$, at which time the IRA investor will be subject to taking an annual required minimum distribution (RMD). In most cases, the Uniform Table is used to determine how the IRA balance must be distributed. However, if a spouse is more than 10 years younger than the account holder, the balance is distributed using the True Joint Life Expectancy and Last Survivor Expectancy Table. If the full minimum distribution is not taken when required, a 50% penalty will be assessed on the amount not taken.

Traditional IRA contributions are fully tax deductible to the amount allowed by law. Additional contributions may be made, but are non-deductible. Withdrawals may begin at age 59$\frac{1}{2}$ without incurring a 10% early withdrawal penalty. However, regular income taxes on withdrawals will apply.

In a Roth IRA, there is no age restriction for contributions, only the requirement that the account holder have earned income. And there is no rule regarding required minimum distributions at age 70$\frac{1}{2}$. Distributions on principle can be taken at any time and distributions on earnings can be taken after five years if certain conditions are met. Roth IRA contributions are not tax deductible, but the distributions are tax exempt.

To the extent that a Roth IRA owner is less than age 59$\frac{1}{2}$ at the time he/she receives a non-qualified distribution, the taxable portion of the distribution (i.e. earnings) will be subject to the 10% early withdrawal penalty.

Funds may be withdrawn from either type of IRA account without penalty for any of the following reasons:

• Attaining age 59$\frac{1}{2}$
• Death
• Disability
• Substantially equal periodic payments (SEPPs)
• Medical expenses in excess of 7.5% of AGI
• Health insurance premiums paid by unemployed individuals
• Distributions paid directly to the IRS due to an IRS levy
• Qualified higher education expenses
• Qualified first-time home buyer expenses

Finding Investment Money

Now, you may be thinking that all this saving and investing sounds good, but where is the money going to come from? Some money may come from adjustments in current living habits. Other funds may come from using existing resources in a different way.

Some ideas for generating investment funds include:

- Living within your means and saving the balance between income and expenses. There are specific suggestions for reducing expenses in the section titled "Spend Less Than Income" in the chapter on Fundamentals of Financial Planning.
- Taking advantage of tax refunds. If you tend to set up your withholding to provide a tax refund, consider putting the refund money into a retirement account.
- Saving a portion of any salary or wage increases. If you were able to live within your means prior to a wage increase, you should be able to continue using the old salary amount to cover expenses and put at least part of the increase toward savings.
- Working to pay off consumer debt (car loan, credit cards, mortgage). As you pay off the debts, continue to make the same monthly payments, but make them to yourself and your retirement account.

Build your nest egg – the earlier the better

It is important to begin saving now, whether you are in your 20's or in your 50's, to take advantage of compounding interest.

The longer you wait, the more opportunities you miss to build your nest egg. The following illustration clearly shows the advantage to starting early in your saving habits. However, there is great value to saving even if you get a late start, and even if you gain no interest at all. You will still have greater financial flexibility and freedom than someone who has not accumulated savings.

Early Saver

Save from age 20 to 60	40 years
Annual Contribution	$2000
Annual Interest	7%
Total Future Value- age 60	$427,220

Total Future Value	=	$427,220
Total contributions	=	80,000
Earnings Growth	=	**347,220**

Late Saver

Save from age 40 to 60	20 years
Annual Contribution	$4000
Annual Interest	7%
Total Future Value- age 60	$175,460

Total Future Value	=	$175,460
Total contributions	=	80,000
Earnings Growth	=	**95,460**

Retirement is not an end, but a new beginning.

Life has many facets, and a good retirement plan will look at a variety of issues. One factor to consider is the ever-increasing potential life span. It's not uncommon to spend over one quarter of one's life in retirement. For those born in 2006, the projected average life span is 75 years for men and 80 years for women.

The longer you live, the longer the projected life span becomes. A 40 year old man today can expect to live another 38 years (a total of 78) and a 40 year old woman can expect to live another 42 years (to 82). By 60, a man can anticipate a life span of 81 years, and a woman 84 years. Once reaching 90, a man's potential life span increases to 94 and a woman's to 95. Given that potential for so many years in retirement, it is very important to plan ahead.

As we age, we often find ourselves with increasing financial responsibilities. Those sandwich years find us struggling with issues that span multiple generations. It is not unusual for young adult children to stay longer in their parents' home or to return home to live with parents during times of financial hardship. There may still be younger kids at home or in college when our parents start to need help. Some elderly parents may not have planned well for their own retirement and now need help with living expenses or assistance with household tasks.

Be cautious in overextending yourself for either your parents or your children. Your money needs to last as long as you live. If your parents have limited resources, they may be eligible for outside assistance that will not compromise your own ability to save for future expenses. The message is not to ignore your children or your parents, but to assist in a reasonable and responsible manner. Sacrificing your own financial security only creates additional problems and will ultimately make things worse for all involved.

There is no reason to stop saving once you retire. Continue to invest. Diversify your assets, preserve them and let them grow.

Pay attention to your asset allocation through periodic review of your investments. A general rule of thumb in determining asset allocation is to assume you will live to be 100. Subtract your current age from 100 and use that number as the percentage of your portfolio to have invested in stocks. Don't panic during stock market corrections. Stick to your objectives and stay the course.

Another important area to consider is long term health care (nursing home coverage). Check into long-term care insurance; just be aware that premiums are not cheap. Since nursing home care can be $85,000 or more a year, the insurance might be worth the cost.

It is important to know that skilled nursing care is different from nursing home coverage. Medicare does not cover nursing home care. It covers only skilled nursing care in a nursing care facility for up to 100 days during the benefit period. All services are covered for the first 20 days, and the next 80 days are paid by Medicare coinsurance. The insured individual pays all costs after the 100 day limit. Your personal family history, lifestyle and current health should be factored into your decision regarding long term health care coverage.

To make the most of your retirement years, remember to maintain a balanced lifestyle. Stay involved socially and mentally. Be conscientious about your diet and exercise. Take good care of yourself and you will significantly enhance enjoyment of your retirement years.

How much do I need to retire?

"How much is enough?" is a common question. The answer depends on each individual's unique life circumstances and anticipated needs and wants for the retirement years. How long you have before your anticipated retirement age, your current health and family longevity all play a role in projecting "how much". There are several items to review, evaluate, and discuss that will help define how much will be needed to achieve the desired goals for life in retirement.

Start by looking at your current financial situation. How much of your monthly income is being used to cover monthly expenses? How much have you already saved, and how is it invested? What is your risk tolerance, and do your investments match your level of comfort? Do you have significant debt? If yes, do you have a plan to pay it off prior to retirement? What are your spending habits and priorities?

What will your needs and wants look like during retirement? (Don't ignore the inflation factor!) Will your spending priorities change? Will you be doing things that require more or less money than you are spending now? What will the monthly expenses look like? How much do you need saved to cover those monthly expenses? There are many internet resources for calculating retirement needs, such as http://money.cnn.com/retirement, http://www.kiplinger.com/tools/retirement-savings-calculator.html. or http://moneycentral.msn.com/Retire/Planner.aspx, You will need to plug in some numbers based on the calculations you've made regarding future needs, as well as provide information on what you've accumulated so far.

Once you've given some thought to identifying that future monthly budget and figured out how much you'll need to save, you may discover you need to step up your savings a notch or two. And you may be wondering how to find more money for saving. We've covered some suggestions for freeing up extra cash in our section on Spend Less than Income in the chapter on Fundamentals of Financial Planning.

So, back to the beginning, how much do you need for retirement? One way to approach that question is to apply some basic formula assumptions and use that information to see how it might apply to your situation. Below are some illustrations that may serve as a wake-up call to get you motivated to begin your retirement savings program. These examples are for illustrations purposes only.

Keep in mind that in addition to the inflation factor, your individual income, spending and saving habits, current investments, and net worth need to be considered when determining your retirement needs. When it comes to retirement planning, one size (or solution) does not fit all situations. Each individual is responsible for determining his or her own needs and planning accordingly. As always, it is helpful to consult with a good financial professional to assist with your personal needs assessment.

Retirement Needs Illustration I

(Wake-up call)

Assuming:

- an inflation rate of 3.5%
- an investment return rate of 7%
- and current annual income of $35,500

One accepted wage replacement ratio is 80% (meaning you will need the equivalent of 80% of your current income in your retirement years).

- 80% of $35,500 is $28,400

Factoring in an anticipated annual Social Security income of $14,000, you would need to generate an additional $14,400 annually (in today's dollars) to meet your retirement needs. How much you will need to save in order to reach that goal depends on how old you are now and how much longer you have to work.

We'll look at some additional assumptions:

Current Age	30	35	50
Retirement Age	65	65	65
Life Expectancy	86	86	86
Years To Retirement (YTR)	35	30	15
Years In Retirement	21	21	21
Capital Needs At Retirement	$737,608	$621,055	$370,702
Currently Saved	-0-	-0-	-0-
Need To Save/Month (NTS)	$445	$548	$1230
YTR x 12 mo/yr x NTS= TC	35x12x$445	30x12x$548	15x12x$1230
Total Contribution(TC)	$186,900	$197,280	$221,400

Note in the italicized line above, we take the number of years to retirement (YTR) and multiply that times twelve to get the number of months to retirement. Then we multiply the number of months to retirement times the amount needed to be saved (NTS) each month to get the total contribution (TC) for each age category on the chart.

As you can see, the younger you are, the more capital you will ultimately need for retirement to counter the effects of inflation. However, the earlier you start, the less you will need to be setting aside each month in order to achieve the desired outcome. In addition, your total out of pocket contribution will be significantly less (as indicated on the bottom line of the chart). Since beginning with different assumptions will lead to very different outcomes, we have presented another set of assumptions below.

Retirement Needs Illustration II

Assuming:

- an inflation rate of 4%
- an investment return rate of 9%
- and current annual income of $62,000
- the 80% replacement wage ratio = $49,600 ($62,000 x .80)

We will again assume a Social Security income of $14,500 per year. This means you would need to generate an additional $35,100 to bring your annual income to the $49,600 determined in the wage replacement ratio. The following chart completes the assumptions for this illustration.

Current Age	35	45	55
Retirement Age	66	66	66
Life Expectancy	86	86	86
Years To Retirement (YTR)	31	21	11
Years In Retirement	20	20	20
Capital Needs At Retirement	$1,572,038	$1,062,015	$717,460
Currently Saved	-0-	-0-	-0-
Required Annual Savings	$10,510	$18,709	$40,857
Need To Save/Month (NTS)	$875	$1560	$3405
YTR x 12 mo/yr x NTS= TC	31x12x$875	21x12x$1560	11x12x$3405
Total Contribution(TC)	$325,500	$393,120	$449,460

Now let's assume that you have already accumulated $60,000 in retirement savings. The reduction in the amount that must be saved to reach the desired goal is shown in the chart below.

Annual Saving Required	$4709	$12,252	$32,040
Monthly Saving Required	$392	$1021	$2670

As noted earlier, those who begin saving earlier have a distinct advantage over those who wait. However, the best time for anyone to start saving is now, no matter what age or how close to retirement.

CHAPTER FOUR

INSURANCE PLANNING

Maung Win

Insurance is a financial planning instrument which can address family protection, wealth transfer, and philanthropy. Insurance as a protection planning instrument is discussed in the first part of this chapter while life insurance for wealth transfer is at the end of the chapter. Wealth transfer and philanthropy will be discussed more thoroughly in later chapters. Here, we will look at insurance as a protection planning instrument.

An effective insurance plan ensures dependents will have adequate support in case of a disability to, or the premature death of, an income earner or homemaker. Insurance also provides protection from unexpected financial disasters. Don't get caught without it! It is best to buy now, because the younger you are, the less expensive insurance will be to purchase.

There are several types of family protection that need to be considered. These include:

• Home

- Auto
- Health
- Umbrella (extended liability coverage above and beyond home owner and auto policy limits)
- Life (such as term, whole, universal, and variable life)
- Disability
- Long-term Care

Insurance is essentially a risk-management tool.

Buying an insurance policy allows the holder to share the risk, and therefore the potential losses, with a group. An individual pays a premium to insure against an unlikely but potentially catastrophic risk. If the catastrophic loss were to occur, insurance would minimize what could be a major financial loss.

Risk management involves making informed choices among various methods of handling risk. To be considered an efficient choice for dealing with risk, insurance must be justified based on a cost/benefit analysis.

To minimize the impact of risks that could cause catastrophic loss, financial planning addresses the following areas:

- Risk to the person
  - Risk of health-related problem, including disability and long-term care
  - Risk of untimely death
- Risk to property
  - Home
  - Auto

- Risk of liability
  - Personal liability
  - Professional liability
  - Umbrella

Risk to the Person

Tools used to manage risk to the person include health, life and disability insurance. In general, insurance makes the most sense when the premiums are relatively low and the precipitating event is fairly unlikely but would be financially devastating.

Health insurance is an exception in that premiums are not low, and many people will find themselves in need of expensive health care. The health and financial consequences of not having health insurance can be severe, so most will opt to have at least catastrophic insurance to protect themselves and their families.

In the past, the elderly have depended on younger generations to provide long term care for their parents and/or grandparents. As this is becoming less typical for families today, Long Term Care insurance is becoming an important tool for protection. Long Term Care policy coverage can include custodial care, home health care, assisted-living care and nursing home care.

Accident and disability insurance should also be considered. During the working years, chance of a disability loss is greater than the chance of an untimely death by about 10 to 1. Yet personal disability insurance is probably the least understood and least utilized tool for personal risk management.

Disability insurance provides benefits in the form of periodic payments for a person who is unable to work due to sickness or injury. Disability insurance can come in many variations:

1. Either group or individual coverage is available. While group disability might be provided through an employer, you may still want to consider an individual disability policy to ensure protection in case disability occurs.
2. Disability income benefit periods may provide payouts for short-term or long-term time frames.
3. If eligible, Social Security Disability benefits may be obtained. Disability policies may coordinate policy benefits with payouts received from Social Security Disability.

Retirees do not need disability coverage, since they no longer have earned income to replace. For those who do need long-term disability coverage, the policy should be non-cancelable or guaranteed renewable with a competitive premium.

In 2009, my daughter, Cynthia Win, had an unfortunate, but real personal experience with the impact of disability income insurance. Cynthia suffered an accident and now is quadriplegic, which has significantly affected her ability to earn an income. In addition to her loss of income, her medical bills have increased greatly due to additional needed care.

Cynthia is covered by her company disability insurance policy and has been collecting the long term disability insurance income provided by that policy. This income alone is not enough to cover all her medical bills and living expenses.

Ten years ago, Cynthia had the foresight to purchase her own disability insurance policy, paying the premiums out of her own pocket. This has allowed her to draw income from both the company policy and her own personal policy. Unlike the disability income derived from her workplace policy, she does not have to pay taxes on the disability benefit from the self-purchased disability insurance policy.

If you are covered by an employer's disability insurance policy, you will lose that benefit if employment is terminated. Therefore, if at all feasible, it is prudent to carry your own disability policy in addition to employer-provided disability insurance.

Generally, it is appropriate to buy disability insurance at a younger age because it is possible to lock in a level premium; one that will not increase as you get older. If purchased at an older age, disability insurance premiums will be significantly higher.

Risk to Property

It is important to have appropriate coverage for your home and auto. Losses in either area can be financially devastating.

Risk of Liability

Personal liability, professional liability and umbrella coverage can be important to protect from lawsuits. It is good risk management to have these in place, especially when in a profession with greater potential risk.

Estimating Life Insurance Needs

It's important to go through a careful analysis of your family's situation in order to accurately estimate your life insurance needs. Be sure to consult with a knowledgeable, reliable, independent insurance agent.

Term life is very valuable coverage for those with children and, in most cases, may be the most appropriate option. It is more affordable than whole life, which would allow one to more easily purchase greater coverage. When purchasing term life insurance, seek a policy that is non-cancelable, guaranteed renewable, with a level premium. Both parents should be covered, even if only one works outside of the home. While most people understand the need to replace wages of the primary breadwinner, the cost to replace a primary care giver can also be significant. It may be necessary to pay for childcare, home-making, and meal preparation; responsibilities that had been the purview of the care giver.

There are different ways to calculate the amount of insurance needed to provide for your loved ones, and it is important to take careful consideration of your family's needs in estimating the appropriate amount of coverage. Again, be sure to consult with a reliable insurance agent.

The following two examples for estimating life insurance needs are just guidelines. Each individual should complete a careful analysis for his/her specific family situation. It is important to realize that the surviving spouse may need to seek employment at an appropriate time to support additional family needs.

1. A rough estimate of insurance needs = ten times the taxpayer's income

   (i.e. Taxpayer's income of $40,000/yr x 10 years = $400,000)

2. Human Life percentage Calculation

$100,000	Gross Pay
(20,000)	Income Tax (Federal & State)
(7,650)	Social Security
(10,000)	Savings, Other Deductions
$ 62,350	Net Pay
$ 12,470	20% of $62,350 – Taxpayer's Consumption
$ 49,880	Net to Survivors (0.4988)

Taxpayer's income of $40,000/yr x 30 years = $1,200,000
Insurance Needs = $1,200,000 x 0.4988 = **$598,560**

Wealth Transfer

Insurance can also be used as a tool in the wealth replacement process by taking advantage of estate and income tax benefits available in setting up certain trusts. A trust can serve multiple purposes of providing an income stream for the donor, eliminating tax liability to beneficiaries, and being a vehicle for charitable giving, which will be discussed in a later chapter.

Wealth Transfer Process Using Arbitrage Strategy

Caution: This process requires a Financial Planner or Advisor with special knowledge in this area.

The following wealth transfer strategy allowed my wife, Rosemarie, to turn a $100,000 investment into a tax-free benefit of $200,000 to our heirs. This is an example of how life insurance can be used as a wealth replacement tool.

1 Rosemarie invested $100,000 in a Single Premium Immediate Annuity (SPIA) that provides a monthly payout for life.

2 She uses part of the monthly payout to pay premiums for a $200,000 life insurance policy. The difference between the SPIA payout and the life insurance premium provides extra income each month. In addition, the life insurance premium is used toward our annual gift tax exclusion.

3 An Irrevocable Life Insurance Trust (ILIT) was created, which removed the $200,000 asset out of our estate.

4 Upon Rosemarie's death, our beneficiaries will receive $200,000 income- tax free.

Life Insurance for Wealth Transfer and Philanthropy

Another strategy involved a client buying a two million dollar insurance policy and creating an ILIT (Irrevocable Life Insurance Trust). Upon death of the client, the proceeds of the ILIT will be outside of the estate, and the beneficiaries will receive the two million dollars tax-free. Beneficiaries may be loved ones as well as designated charities. In this case, the client designated one million to charities and one million to family members.

CHAPTER FIVE

IRA PLANNING FOR FAMILY FORTUNE TAX ADVANTAGE OF STRETCH IRA

Robert Keebler

For many, qualified retirement assets represent a substantial portion of their wealth. Balances within IRAs[1] have grown substantially and will likely continue to grow. The benefits afforded by allowing assets to grow in a tax-deferred environment gives rise to tremendous wealth accumulation during the life of the owner and if structured properly, will give rise to tremendous wealth accumulation for the owner's family. This chapter will discuss and illustrate the power of allowing retirement assets to grow in a tax deferred environment and how retirement assets can be structured to provide the greatest benefit.

Failure to properly structure an IRA may result in the loss of the benefits afforded by tax deferral, namely additional accumulation in a tax-free environment. Thus, it is imperative that the IRA be structured to minimize income tax. The Stretch IRA Concept recognizes this objective, maximizing the legislative

---

1. Throughout this chapter we will generally make reference to IRAs, as IRAs typically allow for the greatest amount of flexibility for planning purposes.

grace allowed in the tax code. Prior to explaining the Stretch IRA Concept, we should first review the IRA distribution provisions of the law.

Basic IRA Distribution Rules

The law allows a taxpayer to contribute pre-tax dollars to an IRA, which may continue to grow on a tax-deferred basis. Upon distribution of the IRA assets, the distribution will be taxed as ordinary income of the recipient. Congress intended that IRAs be used as retirement rather than as general wealth accumulation vehicles. Thus, rules were created that require certain amounts of the IRA to be distributed after the IRA owner reaches a specified age.

The date by which a taxpayer must begin forced distributions is known as the "Required Beginning Date" (RBD). This is generally defined as the April 1st following the calendar year in which a taxpayer reaches age $70^1/_2$.[2] The failure to take a required distribution will result in a 50 percent penalty on the amount that should have been distributed. A taxpayer's life expectancy factor is determined in one of two ways:

1. If the sole beneficiary is the taxpayer's spouse, the "applicable period" is the longer of the distribution period determined under the "Uniform Table" or the true joint life expectancy table (which uses the participant's and spouse's ages in the distribution year). In other words, if the sole beneficiary is the spouse and the spouse is more than 10 years younger than the taxpayer, the true joint life expectancy of the taxpayer and his/her spouse is used. Otherwise, the Uniform Table is used.

---

2. Note that in the case of a qualified plan, the qualified plan participant who owns five percent or less of the entity under which the qualified plan operates does not reach his or her required beginning date until such time as he or she retires.

2. If the sole beneficiary is anyone other than a spouse who is more than 10 years younger than the participant, the "Uniform Table" is used.

A taxpayer's applicable life expectancy factor is utilized to calculate his "Required Minimum Distribution" (RMD) in the following fashion:

$$\text{Required Minimum Distribution} = \frac{\text{Prior Year December 31}^{\text{st}}\ \text{IRA Balance}}{\text{Life Expectancy Factor}}$$

For example, assume that a taxpayer is age 72 and has an IRA balance on December 31st of the previous year of $150,000 and a life expectancy factor of 25.6. His RMD for this year would be $5,859 ($150,000 / 25.6).

Choice of Beneficiary

The rules allow a taxpayer to choose a beneficiary based solely on whom he wants to leave the death benefits to. There is no concern that leaving benefits to the beneficiary who is the best choice for post-death distributions will accelerate required distributions to the participant during his life.

Designated Beneficiary

For post death required minimum distributions, it must be possible to identify an age in order to calculate a life expectancy factor. Therefore, the designated beneficiary must generally be an individual with a determinable life expectancy.

A beneficiary is the person, persons or entity that will receive the remaining balance in the IRA or qualified retirement plan upon a taxpayer's death. However, for IRAs and qualified retirement plans it is critical that the beneficiaries qualify under the law as a "designated beneficiary". Only individuals and certain types of trusts qualify under the law as a "designated beneficiary". Estates and charities do not. The failure to have a designated beneficiary will result in either of the following:

1. If a taxpayer dies before his RBD, the IRA must be distributed no later than December 31st of the fifth anniversary year of his death, or

2. If a taxpayer dies after his RBD, the IRA must be distributed based upon his life expectancy in the year of death. This factor is reduced by one for each succeeding year.

Thus, it is critical that a qualified designated beneficiary be named.

Required distributions to the beneficiaries who inherit the benefits are based on the life expectancies of those beneficiaries. The designated beneficiary is determined based on the beneficiaries designated as of the last day of the calendar year following the calendar year of the employee's death. Any person who was a beneficiary as of the date of a taxpayer's death, but is not a beneficiary as of that later date (e.g., because the person disclaims entitlement to the benefit to which the person is entitled before that date) is not taken into account in determining a taxpayer's designated beneficiary for purposes of determining the distribution period for RMDs after his death. Post-death distributions are taken out over the life expectancy of the designated beneficiary by referencing the Single Life Table of Treas. Reg. § 1.72-9.

Spouse as Designated Beneficiary

If a taxpayer designates his/her spouse as beneficiary, there are several favorable options not available to other designated beneficiaries.

If the spouse is the beneficiary, the RMDs can be deferred until the end of the calendar year in which the taxpayer would have attained age 70$\frac{1}{2}$ had death not occurred. If the surviving spouse dies before the distributions begin, the rules will be applied as if he/she were the owner and died before the RBD. This means that a new determination of who is the designated beneficiary of the now-deceased surviving spouse will be made as of December 31 following the year of the surviving spouse's death. Benefits will be distributed based on the life expectancy of the surviving spouse's beneficiary.

When the surviving spouse, as beneficiary, begins receiving minimum distributions, life expectancy is recalculated each year. Upon the spouse's death, the remaining plan balance is then distributed over a fixed number of years representing the spouse's life expectancy as determined by age at the birthday in the year of death. This new proposed regulation, a combination of recalculation and fixed term methods, provides two benefits. First, recalculation of life expectancy during the spouse's lifetime provides an income for life, if the spouse is taking just required minimum distributions each year. Second, the fixed term method of determining the spouse's remaining life expectancy at the time of death provides a period of time for the beneficiaries to prorate their inheritance.

An option only available to a spouse as beneficiary is the rollover option. Whether the surviving spouse is the only beneficiary or one of several beneficiaries, he/she can roll the pro rata share into either a new or existing traditional IRA.

The following three examples illustrate the consequences of three situations: (1) death of the surviving spouse before the RBD and rollover election, (2) death of the surviving spouse after the RBD and no rollover election, and (3) death of the surviving spouse after the rollover election but before the RBD.

Example 1

John and his wife, Jane, are the same age. John dies at age 45. Jane is the sole beneficiary of his IRA. She decides to leave the IRA in John's name. At age 57, Jane dies. At the beneficiary determination date, her son, the beneficiary, can take distributions over his life expectancy. Because the son was age 28 in the year following the year of his mother's death, he can "stretch" his inheritance over 55.3 years.

Example 2

John and his wife, Jane, are the same age. John dies at age 45. Jane is the sole beneficiary of his IRA. She decides to leave the IRA in John's name. At age 72, Jane dies. Distributions to Jane's son, the beneficiary, will be based on Jane's remaining life expectancy, 15.5 years.

Example 3

John and his wife, Jane, are the same age. John dies at age 45. Jane is the sole beneficiary of his IRA. She decides to leave the IRA in John's name. At age 59$^{1}/_{2}$, Jane rolls John's IRA into a new IRA in her name and designates her son as the beneficiary. Jane dies at age 68. Distributions to her son will be based on his life expectancy. Since the son was age 39, his life expectancy is 44.6 years. Therefore, he can "stretch" his inheritance over 44.6 years.

As the above three points illustrate, an important strategy is to keep the IRA in the name of the deceased spouse until the surviving spouse attains age $59^1/_2$. Then a rollover should be executed. This strategy provides two important benefits. First, a surviving spouse who is younger than $59^1/_2$ can take distributions from the deceased spouse's IRA without incurring the 10 percent federal penalty tax. Second, executing a rollover at age $59^1/_2$ allows the surviving spouse to name new beneficiaries so that if death occurs after the RBD, distributions to the beneficiaries will be based on their life expectancy as opposed to the shorter life expectancy of the IRA owner.

Multiple Beneficiaries

If there are multiple beneficiaries where "separate accounts" were not established, and all are individuals (even if one is the spouse), the beneficiaries must take distributions over the oldest beneficiary's life expectancy. This determination is made based on the beneficiary's age on his/her birthday in the year of the first distribution. For each succeeding year, this factor is reduced by one. Distributions must begin no later than December 31st of that same year. If a taxpayer died after his required beginning date, a RMD must be taken for the year of his death based upon his age in the year of death.

If the IRA is segregated into "separate accounts" by December 31st of the year following the year of the account owner's death, each beneficiary can independently calculate his/her RMDs based on their individual life expectancy.

The creation of "separate accounts" is particularly valuable if there is a beneficiary who is not an individual. Such a beneficiary would typically result in the owner being treated as having "no designated beneficiary". However, if the account is segregated by December 31st of the year following the year of the account owner's death, only the "account" with the non-designated beneficiary would be subject to the unfavorable RMDs previously discussed.

Year of Death Distribution

If a taxpayer dies on or after his RBD, the minimum distribution for the year in which he dies is based on his required distribution schedule. If the deceased owner had not yet taken the minimum distribution for the year of death, the beneficiaries must take out that distribution before the end of the year in which the death occurred.

Recognition of the above facts provides the basis for the Stretch IRA Concept.

STRETCH IRA CONCEPT

The Stretch IRA Concept contemplates arranging a taxpayer's assets in such a way that the balance in an IRA can be inherited intact by beneficiaries or a trust for their benefit. As previously discussed, the key advantage of this strategy is that it allows the beneficiaries to keep the IRA in a tax-deferred environment. If properly executed, this strategy can create substantial wealth transfer opportunities for a taxpayer's family.

With the uncertainty that exists over the changes in both state and federal gift and estate tax laws, one of the primary objectives of a taxpayer's estate and retirement distribution planning will be to build in flexibility. One of the most valuable tools for modifying an estate and retirement distribution plan to meet any changes in needs or objectives is the careful and strategic use of a disclaimer. The following structure is designed to allow the surviving spouse the ability to choose among the following possibilities:

- Retirement plan assets will pass to the surviving spouse as a direct beneficiary, and he or she will be allowed to roll those assets into a new IRA and name the beneficiaries of his or her choice of that IRA.

- In the event of a disclaimer, retirement account assets will pass to a stand-alone trust that includes the surviving spouse as a beneficiary who will receive the financial protection provided by those assets while allowing the assets to be protected from future tax by full use of the deceased spouse's unified credit.

- In the event of a second disclaimer, retirement account assets will pass to a stand-alone trust for the benefit of children, allowing the children to take required distributions based upon the oldest child's life expectancy.

To make this strategy work, both the beneficiary designation and the trust that may become the beneficiary must be carefully drafted to comply with the complex tax rules that qualify the trust as a potential beneficiary and allow the disclaimer to have its intended effect. Provided that this is done, the strategy will work. Of course, the plan must be carefully structured to accomplish the objectives.

- First, the Beneficiary Designation Form must provide that although the surviving spouse is the primary beneficiary, in the event that he/she disclaims his/her interest, it will be paid to the trust for the benefit of spouse and children.

- The trust for the benefit of spouse and children must be set up to qualify as a designated beneficiary and provide that beneficial distributions of income or principal or both may be made to the surviving spouse.

- The Beneficiary Designation Form must provide that in the event that the surviving spouse disclaims his/her beneficiary interest in the trust the retirement asset proceeds will be paid in separate shares to the children, or in the alternative to qualifying trusts for their benefit.

Each scenario has its own potential benefits, which can be chosen, depending upon the laws and priorities in existence at the first spouse's death. These include the following:

Scenario One: *The surviving spouse does not disclaim*

If the surviving spouse does not disclaim the retirement account, he/she will be the beneficiary. He/she will then have complete discretion to make withdrawals based upon his/her needs and income tax circumstances. The retirement account will have minimum distributions calculated each year based upon the surviving spouse's life expectancy in that year. This strategy will therefore produce lower required minimum distributions and therefore a larger benefit from tax deferred growth within the retirement account than the second scenario.

In addition, the surviving spouse will be able to name new beneficiaries for the retirement account who will inherit their shares upon the surviving spouse's death. If the surviving spouse carefully sets up his/her beneficiary designations, the new beneficiaries, who will most likely be children, will be allowed to take distributions from their shares of the retirement account over their own individual life expectancies.

The surviving spouse would also be able to roll over the account into an account set up and maintained in his/her name. This will allow the surviving spouse to take distributions based on his/her life expectancy and name new beneficiaries who will take distributions based on their life expectancies upon the surviving spouse's death.

Scenario Two: The surviving spouse disclaims all or a portion of the account

If the surviving spouse enters a single disclaimer, he/she will no longer be the sole beneficiary of the retirement account and will not be able to roll the account over to treat it as his/her own. However, the retirement account will now be paid to the trust that will be able to use the deceased spouse's available unified credit. If the retirement account is paid to this trust, it will not be subject to death or transfer tax upon the surviving spouse's death, no matter what changes Congress makes to the tax rates or the exemptions and credits.

The payments from the retirement account can be used for the benefit of the surviving spouse and the children, or if the grantor chooses, the assets of the Trust can also be used for the benefit of other family members.

Minimum distributions will be calculated based upon the surviving spouse's life expectancy in the year following the year of the deceased spouse's death. Because other persons are also beneficiaries (the children), calculations will use the first year factor reduced by one for each subsequent year. After the surviving spouse's death, required distributions will continue to be calculated based upon his/her life expectancy.

This scenario allows the retirement account to be used for the benefit of the surviving spouse, but still protected from further estate or transfer tax. It should be given strong consideration if the deceased spouse dies without other assets that can be used to take full advantage of his/her unified credit exemption equivalent.

The surviving spouse would not have to disclaim the entire retirement account, but instead could disclaim only a portion of the account. The portion not disclaimed could be rolled over into a retirement account, set up, and maintained in the surviving spouse's name.

Scenario Three: The surviving spouse disclaims twice

If the surviving spouse disclaims his/her interest as direct beneficiary, as well as his/her interest in the trust, the beneficiary designation may provide that the retirement account will then be paid either directly to the children (or grandchildren) or to the trust solely for the children's benefit.

In this scenario, not only may the full unified credit equivalent be used, but also the retirement account will have required distributions based upon the age of the oldest child. This will usually produce the lowest required distributions and therefore the largest benefit from the continued tax deferral of the investments in these accounts.

Since the surviving spouse will receive no benefits under this scenario, the "double disclaimer" strategy will only be used where he/she has other assets to provide for his/her financial needs. When this strategy is employed, the value of the wealth transferred is greatly enhanced by the lengthy deferral of withdrawal that is possible when younger individuals are named as beneficiaries.

Tremendous wealth accumulation can be achieved through the Stretch IRA Concept. If properly executed, this strategy can create substantial wealth transfer opportunities for a plan owner's family. Consider for example, a $500,000 IRA under four differing scenarios, ranging from immediate liquidation of the entire IRA to stretching distributions over the youngest beneficiary's life expectancy. Assuming an 8% growth rate, a 35% federal income tax rate, a 50% turnover on growth and a 15% federal capital gains rate, the power of the Inherited IRA concept is illustrated below:

Year	Immediate Distribution	IRA Payable to Non-Qualified Designated Beneficiary (ie. 5-Year Rule)	IRA Payable to 40 Year Old Non-Spousal Beneficiary	IRA Payable to 15 Year Old Non-Spousal Beneficiary
2010	$321,600	$540,000	$540,000	540,000
2015	455,292	472,536	755,047	768,934
2020	644,561	668,973	1,050,081	1,091,948
2025	912,510	947,071	1,451,599	1,546,147
2030	1,291,849	1,340,777	1,992,846	2,182,420
2035	1,828,882	1,898,150	2,714,100	3,070,715
2040	2,589,164	2,687,228	3,661,659	4,302,715
2045	3,665,503	3,804,332	4,884,195	6,005,532

As is evident from this example, by properly structuring the IRA, over the course of 35 years, an additional after-tax amount of over $2,000,000 could have been passed to the beneficiaries. Properly structuring beneficiary designations offers a tremendous opportunity for those taxpayers who have had the foresight to accumulate wealth in a tax-deferred vehicle.

After Win attended seminars by Bob Keebler and discussed his options with estate planning attorney Foss Hooper, Win decided to use a revocable standalone IRA trust as the beneficiary of his IRA. Win did this for both wealth accumulation and asset protection reasons. In other words, he gets to have his cake and eat it too. For wealth accumulation the trust was designed to use the individual life expectancies of each of Win & Rosemarie's children. For asset protection the trust will keep the IRAs from being subject to estate tax at the beneficiary's death, and protect the beneficiary's IRA from lawsuits and bankruptcy.

CHAPTER SIX

ESTATE PLANNING

• Effective arrangement of care for family members
• Efficient transfer of wealth to beneficiaries

Edward F. Hooper

What is meant by estate planning?

Estate planning is not just about documents and probate. Likewise, it's not just about death and taxes. Good estate planning is a process that allows you to control your wealth while you are alive; protect yourself and your loved ones; distribute your property at death to who you want in the manner you wish; and to do all of that at the lowest cost of administration. Good estate planning keeps you and your loved ones in charge and addresses many non-financial issues in addition to the traditional financial ones. The remainder of this chapter answers common questions and provides more detail to assist you in determining whether or not your current plan is adequate.

When is the best time to do estate planning?

Now is the best time. Many people wait to do estate planning until a certain event such as the birth of children or retirement. The problem with that approach is that you can never predict the future and the consequences to yourself and your loved ones. If you either become disabled or die, without a well crafted estate plan, the results can be disastrous.

Do I need an attorney to complete my estate plan?

While it is theoretically possible to remove your own appendix with a razor blade and a bottle of scotch; it is not recommended. Likewise, to do your own estate plan without the advice of an attorney can lead to big trouble. It is true that if everything goes as you hope the estate plan can be fairly simple and short. However, you don't have a crystal ball, and things seldom go according to plan. It may be possible to find computer software to draft your own documents, but rarely does a non-attorney know the necessary formalities for execution of a will. The attorney's job is only partially the drafting of documents. The most valuable part of the attorney's role is the counseling. A good estate planning attorney will know both tax and probate law, and also the questions to ask so that the resulting estate plan tailors the provisions of your estate plan to the uniqueness of your family.

Can any attorney prepare my estate plan?

Any licensed attorney is allowed to draft estate planning documents. However, just as you would not have your family doctor do brain surgery, it is best to leave the drafting of complicated estate planning documents to someone who limits their legal practice to just estate planning. A general practice attorney is not going to know estate planning law well enough to ask the right questions or to properly draft the documents. Estate plans are not something that can be just plucked out of a form book.

What professional advisors need to be involved with my estate plan?

Life is complicated, and it typically takes a team of advisors to cover all of the areas needed to do a complete financial and estate plan. The estate planning attorney will draft the necessary legal documents, but for the documents to work properly your financial assets must be owned properly. This means, if you have a financial planner, that person will need to work with the estate planning attorney. It is also advisable that the person who prepares your taxes be updated about your planning.

Will I have to pay death taxes?

The answer to this depends upon both your level of assets and the actions of Congress. The amount of assets that are allowed to pass free of death taxes has varied considerably in recent years. In the year 2009 you were allowed to pass $3.5 million without a death tax. In 2010, as this chapter is being written, there is no death tax. However, in the year 2011 the tax reappears and only $1 million can pass free of tax. The tax rate starts at 41% and quickly climbs to 55%.

If you are married, the above estate tax exemption amounts can be effectively doubled by setting up a family trust on the first death to use the deceased spouse's pass-free-on-death coupon. This can only be done with a will or trust. Joint ownership and beneficiary designations do not provide a mechanism for protecting the pass free coupon. Also, for married couples, an unlimited amount may pass between spouses without tax as long as the receiving spouse is a US citizen.

Because there is so much possibility for change, two things should be kept in mind. First, your estate planning attorney should draft your estate plan so that you will get the optimal tax result regardless of the current limits. Second, the design of your plan should be based upon the things that you can control. This means that your plan should be built around you and your loved ones needs, not tax considerations. While it is important to minimize taxes, it is also important to not let the tax tail wag the estate planning dog.

How much can I give away during my lifetime?

As life expectancies increase, using lifetime gifts to benefit your loved ones becomes a more important strategy. Years ago people were inheriting in their 40's. Now the age of inheritance is creeping past normal retirement age. As a result many inheritances are too late to make much of an impact. To provide help at the time it is most needed will probably be accomplished through lifetime gifts.

There are two types of gifts: non-taxable and taxable. The amount of non-taxable gifts you can give to each person is indexed for inflation, and during 2010 the maximum for all gifts to any one person is $13,000. As long as you stay within that limit there is nothing that needs to be filed with the IRS. Gifts above the annual exclusion amount may still be made, however they are considered taxable and you will need to file a gift tax return. The first $1,000,000 of taxable gifts is covered by a lifetime exemption and you will not have to pay any gift tax at the time of the gift. Each dollar of your $1,000,000 lifetime exemption that you use will reduce the amount you can leave free of death taxes by one dollar. In other words, from a tax perspective, it makes no difference whether you give someone something during your lifetime or leave it to them at death. Please remember that any gifts made within the annual limit (currently $13,000) do not affect the amount you may leave, tax free, at death.

When you are dealing with an appreciated asset the income tax consequences of lifetime gifts and inheriting at death are different. Ignoring timing considerations, it is better to receive an appreciated asset via inheritance rather than by a lifetime gift. This is because with a gift you carry over the donor's original cost basis and with an inheritance the cost basis is reset to the value on the date of death. Therefore, when you sell the asset you may not need to pay any capital gains tax on an inheritance, but may need to for a gift.

Finally, gifts do not have to be made directly to the intended recipient. Just as with an inheritance, a gift can be made to a trust for the recipient's benefit. There are many reasons for doing this including asset protection and providing assistance to someone who is too young, or who lacks the skills to manage the property.

What are the most common types of estate plans?

The most common estate plan is to do nothing. Unfortunately, this plan gives you the least control and can lead to disastrous results. In real life no one really does nothing. Most people at least use some joint ownership of assets and beneficiary designations (which are the next two common estate plans). The two types of unified estate plans rely on a will or utilize a revocable living trust.

Why can't I just use beneficiary designations?

You can, but it is a very fragmented way to plan. With a will or trust there is one central place where all of the assets are collected and administered. That means one place to pay all expenses and debts, and one place from which to make all distributions. With beneficiary designations each asset is distributed individually. There is no central point of control and no account from which to pay expenses such as funeral bills and taxes. In other words, the beneficiaries will have to "pass the hat" to pay expenses; and good luck getting everyone to chip in.

The other issue with beneficiary designations is that there are limited options for protecting and controlling the distribution. For instance, if a minor is the beneficiary of a life insurance policy, a court appointed guardian will need to manage the asset until the minor turns 18. At that time the proceeds are turned over to the minor with no protections to ensure the funds are used wisely.

What is meant by joint ownership?

When you own property with someone else it will either be as tenants in common or as joint tenants. Tenants in common means that you own an undivided fraction of the entire property and can do whatever you want with it when you die. Tenants in common do not have to own the property equally, and can have acquired their interests at different time.

Joint tenants, on the other hand, own the property equally and acquire their interest at the same time. The legal fiction is that each joint tenant owns 100% of the property. Joint tenancy also comes with a feature called survivorship. What this means is that when a joint tenant dies, his or her interest in the property is extinguished and ownership vests in the remaining joint tenant or tenants. In other words, you have no control over where your joint tenancy interest goes at your death. Because the surviving joint tenant was deemed to own 100% of the property from the beginning, there is no interest to transfer at death and the joint tenancy property passes outside of probate.

What is probate?

Probate is a court proceeding in which a judge decides where your property should go. If you have a will, and it was properly executed and admitted to probate, it will guide the judge. Without a will (a condition called intestacy), State Law will determine how your property is distributed.

Normally a probate proceeding will be started by the person you nominate as Personal Representative in your will. That person will file the necessary paperwork, send a copy of the will to all beneficiaries and heirs at law, and then the court will schedule a hearing date for admission of the will. In most cases, if all of the beneficiaries and heirs at law sign a waiver, the Personal Representative can be appointed without a hearing. At this time Testamentary Letters are issued to the Personal Representative. This is what gives the Personal Representative the power to act on behalf of the estate.

Until a Personal Representative is appointed by the court nothing can be done. Powers of Attorney are no longer valid and there is no access to any of the accounts. In the event something needs to be done quickly, the court may appoint a Special Administrator to carry out specific tasks prior to appointment of the Personal Representative.

The Personal Representative's duties include:

- Publishing a notice to creditors
- Marshalling all of the estate assets
- Paying debts and claims against the estate

- Sending copies of court required documents to the beneficiaries
- Preparing an inventory of assets
- Filing tax returns
- Distributing bequests to the beneficiaries
- Preparing and submitting a final accounting

Why is probate so expensive?

As you can see there is a lot that needs to be done. The probate process takes a lot of time and effort. For an average size estate the legal fees alone will be about 3% of the probate estate. This is two to three times what it normally takes to settle a revocable trust. As with many things in life, you are rewarded for advanced planning. For those who do not plan probate is often the only, and a very expensive, alternative.

What are the parts of an estate plan?

A good estate plan is more than just a will or revocable trust. You also need everything to manage your property during disability, make health care decisions on your behalf, and to distribute your property. As an example, a good estate plan for a married couple should include the following:

- Wills (if using a trust, this is called a pour-over will)
- Revocable Living Trust (unless the plan is will based)
- Durable Powers of Attorney
- Health Care Powers of Attorney
- Living Wills
- Property Agreement

- HIPPA Disclosure Authorizations
- Personal Property Memoranda
- Memorial Instructions
- Assignments of Personal Property
- A Summary Listing of Agents, Personal Representatives and Trustees

Can an estate plan be changed?

Because we cannot predict the future it is important that changes can be made to your estate plan. For documents such as a will, revocable trust and powers of attorney you can make changes as long as you are alive and not incapacitated. If you are incapacitated, changes may be able to be made to a trust with your power of attorney if you so provide in the trust. You will not be able to make changes to your will if you lack testamentary capacity. During incapacity and after death the trust protector, if named in your trust, may make corrective changes.

For irrevocable trusts, and following your death, changes can be made by the beneficiary of a trust share if you included provisions for this in the trust agreement. Otherwise, as a last resort the trust beneficiaries can petition a court to make necessary changes to an irrevocable trust. In some states, if all of the grantors and beneficiaries agree, an irrevocable trust can be changed.

What is the difference between a will and a trust?

Basically a will is a set of instructions to the probate judge on how you want your property to pass. On the other hand, a revocable living trust is a contract between yourself and the trustee that sets up the rules for how your property is to be managed during your lifetime, and what is to happen to the property upon either your disability or death. Unfortunately, most wills don't work as intended because much of the property passes outside the will because of joint ownership and beneficiary designations.

Because the trust itself does not become disabled or die, there is no need to have trust assets go through probate. The key to probate avoidance is to transfer your assets to the trust during your lifetime. This process is called funding the trust. In summary, with a will the judge is in charge and with a funded trust your loved ones are in charge.

Win & Rosemarie decided to use a revocable living trust (RLT), rather than wills, because it provided for asset management during disability and probate avoidance at death. They funded their trust by transferring their accounts into the name of their trust and also changed beneficiary designations to point to the trust. This way Win & Rosemarie's trust provides a single point of control for their assets, and only one place to make changes if needed in the future.

Why can't I use just a simple two page will or trust?

Anyone can develop a short and simple plan that will work properly if everything works as you want. Unfortunately, seldom does everything work as planned. Life is complex and the solutions to life's problems just do not lend themselves to cookie cutter planning. A properly drafted estate plan will not only give the optimum result if everything goes the way you want, but will also give the best result possible under the circumstances no matter what happens in the future. As a result, your estate plan has to have contingencies for anything that could happen. If you are traveling to Florida in the summer it is still a good idea to throw a sweater in the suitcase. You will probably not need it, but as long as it doesn't make things more difficult, why not have it along? Likewise, a good estate plan will be loaded with sweaters that are there just in case.

What are the different types of trusts?

There are multiple ways to classify trusts. The first is by the method that created them. If the trust is set up in your will it is called a testamentary trust. During the probate process the judge establishes the trust, and possibly may supervise it in ensuing years. A trust you set up during your lifetime is called an inter vivos (or living) trust. This type of trust is set up by you and comes into being while you are still alive, without any court involvement. A living trust can be either revocable or irrevocable. Revocable trusts are used as will substitutes to manage your property during your lifetime (including during disability) and to pass your property at death. The property remains fully under your control and you can make changes and also serve as your own trustee. An irrevocable trust, on the other hand, cannot be changed and is used primarily to remove assets from your taxable estate, or to make them non-available for payment of nursing home expenses.

Are there different types of trustees?

The first way to classify trustees is as either corporate or individual. Corporate trustees are professionals such as bank trust departments. An individual trustee is a person such as yourself or a loved one.

Trustees can act alone, in which case they are called sole trustees. When there is more than one acting trustee they are called co-trustees. Depending upon the trust document, the co-trustees may need to act by unanimous vote, majority vote, or any one of the co-trustees may act alone. Allowing a co-trustee to act alone provides the most flexibility, but requiring majority or unanimous vote provides greater security and control.

The trustees who are currently serving are normally called the acting trustees. In the event an acting trustee cannot serve, the trust agreement usually provides for named successor trustees. In addition, trustees may be named or appointed to handle specific tasks such as a distribution trustee.

Who should be the trustee?

The answer to this question depends upon the goals of the person setting up the trust and the qualifications of the pool of potential candidates. In general, if asset protection is not a top priority and there are no dark clouds on the horizon, the trust grantor may act as his or her own trustee, or the beneficiary of a trust share may serve as their own trustee. If more protection is needed, then there should probably be co-trustees and possibly independent trustees. In the event that conflict is likely a corporate trustee should be used.

What is a trust protector?

A trust protector is an independent third party who is empowered to make changes to your trust when you cannot, either because of death or disability. The types of changes include drafting errors, provisions to conform to changes in the law, and changes necessary to clarify trust provisions in order to carry out your intent.

Should I change the name on my accounts to that of my trust?

The process of changing the name on accounts is called

funding the trust. In most cases your assets should be re-titled to the name of your trust. Funding the trust makes it easier for successor trustees to take over and will keep your assets out of probate. Most attorneys will leave it up to you to fund your trust, with the result that most trusts are not properly funded. A good estate planning attorney will view trust funding as part of their job.

What is the purpose of a durable power of attorney?

A financial power of attorney allows someone you designate, your agent, to sign documents on your behalf. The power may become effective immediately upon signing, or "spring" into force upon a finding of disability. Some people are not comfortable giving their agent the power to sign right away. But, why is the agent to be trusted upon disability and not before?

In most states the default for powers of attorney is that they are "durable." The power of attorney agent can, if allowed in the power, perform those acts that the principle could have otherwise performed. But, if the principal is disabled, he or she cannot sign documents, so neither can the agent. The solution is to have the power be durable so that the agent can sign when the principal is incapacitated. Regardless of whether or not the power is durable, it terminates upon the principal's death.

What provisions should be in a power of attorney?

First, make certain the power states that it is durable. Regardless of state law it is a good idea to have this stated in the power. Next, it is recommended that the power be immediate and not springing. Not having to get signed disability certificates from doctors makes it easier for the agent to act. Also, it is not easy to get the power "unsprung" if the disability is only temporary. There are also many times when you might want your power of attorney agent to sign, even though you are not disabled, but merely out of town.

Allowing the power of attorney agent to make gifts is viewed as a "dangerous" power because the agent can use it to transfer your assets. For this reason many State POA forms require an extra step to grant this power. The problem is that without the gifting power it is nearly impossible to do any divestment planning to protect your assets from a prolonged nursing home stay. Therefore, your power of attorney should include gifting provisions, and these provisions should allow gifts beyond the annual gift exclusion limit. If there is a problem with gifting in a power of attorney it is not that the power was granted, but that the wrong agent was chosen.

What are my options for choosing a power of attorney agent?

You can choose a single agent or multiple agents. If there are multiple agents serving the power of attorney should state whether they have to all act together, or if any one of them can act alone. If a single agent is serving, then there should be at least one successor agent named in the power. Usually the named agents are family members or friends, but on occasion a corporate fiduciary, such as a bank trust company, will be named.

What is a health care power of attorney?

In the short term this is the most important part of your estate plan, because it could be a matter of life and death, and time is of the essence. A health care power of attorney is the document in which you name the person who is authorized to make health care decision for you. Usually only one person can serve as your agent, although your power should name backups.

The named health care agent is basically called upon to make two types of decisions. The first one is assisting you when a course of treatment needs to be chosen that is beneficial to you and could extend your life. The other type of decision is sometimes called "pulling the plug." In this case the agent is asked to decide when there is no reasonable hope for your recovery and to remove you from treatment that is futile. Even if a decision is made to remove you from artificial feeding and hydration, it is important that your power specify that you receive enough food and hydration, not to prolong your life, but to keep you comfortable.

It is important that you discuss your feelings with your agent at the time you sign your health care power. This is because your agent is not supposed to make any decisions, but rather to understand your feelings and relay the decisions you have already made to the medical personnel. It is not fair to make your agent guess about what you want and not understanding your wishes can lead to family conflict.

If allowed by your State Law it is best if the health care power of attorney be effective immediately, rather than springing into effect upon your incapacity. Many times when the power is needed the incapacity is temporary, and with a "springing" power it is very difficult to get you back into decision making capability after the temporary disability is past. There are instances where an assisted living facility will not take in someone who has a health care power of attorney that has been "sprung."

The final point about health care powers of attorney is that they need to be accessible. For this reason you should provide your doctor and other health care providers with a copy for your medical records. In addition there are a number of services that will store your power for access via fax or the Internet in the event it is needed and a copy is not readily available. These services give you an ID card for your wallet or purse that lists the service you are using and how to obtain the documents. Imagine being away from home and in an automobile accident. How would the hospital know who to contact and how to get hold of them?

Who should be my health care agent?

This is a case where location really does matter. While some degree of medical knowledge won't hurt; the most important qualification is that your agent knows your wishes and be able to communicate them to the medical staff. It is almost impossible for a child who lives 1,000 or more miles away to do this effectively. Ask yourself, if you were in the hospital, who would be the first one there and who could visit regularly? The answer to this question will give insight as to who your agent should be.

What is the difference between a health care power of attorney and a living will?

In a health care power of attorney you name someone to assist with your medical decisions. The role is that of the family spokesperson. It is the agent's role to communicate your wishes. With a living will there is no person to communicate your wishes. Rather, the document itself tells the medical staff what you wish. As a practical matter the living will is seldom used, and the documents should state, when there is a conflict, which one prevails. Normally, the health care power will trump the living will.

Why do I need a HIPAA authorization?

The HIPPA law restricts to whom the people with your medical information may disclose what is going on. The benefit is that your private information is protected. The down side is that your loved ones, particularly those who live far away, are unable to find out what is going on. It is important that you list those family members and friends who you would like to receive disclosure of your protected information, in a written HIPPA authorization. Just like your health care power, a copy of this authorization should be given to your doctor and any other medical facility you use.

How do I appoint a guardian for my minor children?

Actually, you don't. Only a judge can appoint a guardian, so technically you nominate someone for the judge to appoint. The place to nominate the guardian is in your will. While this works in the event of your death, if you were to become disabled the will has no effect. Therefore, it is also wise to nominate a guardian for your children in your power of attorney in the event you become disabled and cannot take care of them.

Of all the appointments in an estate plan, for most people this is the most difficult decision. No one will be able to take your place, but it is important that you choose, rather than some judge who doesn't know you or your family. If your children are young they will probably live with the guardian. If they are almost adults they may live with the guardian if he or she is located nearby. If the guardian does not live near you they have the option of arranging for a place for your children that would leave them in the same school and not add the loss of friends on top of the loss of a parent.

It is not enough to just name a guardian; you must also provide sufficient funds so that they can raise your children. With the affordability of term life insurance there is no excuse for not having an estate large enough to provide for your children. Typically your estate plan will provide for a single common trust that is used by the guardian to pay all of the costs associated with raising your children. After your children all reach a certain age the estate plan will provide that any funds remaining will be divided into shares for each child.

How do I provide for a beneficiary who is receiving government benefits?

This is a problem because many government benefits are only available to those without any assets. An inheritance could cause the beneficiary to lose those benefits, and need to exhaust the inheritance before again becoming eligible. As a result the beneficiary is no further ahead than if they had been disinherited. In fact, disinheriting the beneficiary was the traditional solution to this problem. Most people found this to be unpalatable.

The proper solution is to use a Special Needs Trust. This type of trust provides benefits but prohibits the trustee from making any distributions that would replace government benefits or would cause disqualification from benefits. It can be drafted so that, if there are no governmental benefits the trust acts just like a general needs trust and the special needs provisions only kick in if the beneficiary becomes otherwise eligible. This type of trust is particularly well suited when leaving assets to someone who is elderly and may be a candidate for nursing home care. Then, if the beneficiary does go into the nursing home the trust assets wouldn't disqualify them from assistance through the Medicaid program.

The type of special needs trust discussed above is called a third party trust because you set them up for someone else. With a third party trust there is no need to include provisions for reimbursing the government after the beneficiary's death for any benefits provided. On the other hand, if the beneficiary's own funds are used to fund the trust, it is call a first party trust and must include pay-back provisions.

What are my choices for leaving property to my children?

Frequently people only consider leaving their property outright to their beneficiaries. While this is the most common approach, it is seldom optimal. In the past the emphasis was always on the sending side of the equation. More recently the trend has started to shift to the wealth reception side. The key issues center around the timing of the bequest and the method of ownership.

One question is; when do I no longer have to protect the beneficiary against himself or herself? People addressing this concern often leave the beneficiary their bequest in trust with staggered distributions at specified ages. This way, it is felt, if the beneficiary messes up with the first distribution at least they have a couple more shots of getting it right.

Another question is; when do I no longer need to worry about protecting the beneficiary against others? The answer to this question is obvious. There is always a need to protect against creditors and predators. To address this concern the inheritance is left to the beneficiary in a lifetime trust. Depending upon the level of protection desired, the beneficiary could be either a co-trustee or even a sole trustee. The trust could be for the beneficiary and any of the beneficiary's descendants. The beneficiary could also be given the power to re-write the terms of the trust as to who gets the share at the beneficiary's death, and how the property will pass.

Many times people have difficulty with the concept of leaving an inheritance in trust. They may feel it is controlling from the grave or that the beneficiary won't have the necessary control or flexibility in managing investments or making distributions. This is not the case. In order to overcome this perception it is important to differentiate between ownership and control. Ownership brings lawsuits. Control brings use and enjoyment.

How do I leave property to a minor?

If there is anything certain in estate planning, it is that you should not leave assets outright to young people. It is not an act of love to put someone in a position where they lack the skill to be successful. Without some real world experience, most people lack the necessary knowledge to successfully manage money. In fact, many young people have had their lives ruined by an inheritance that did not have the proper controls.

People under the age of 18 cannot own property. An outright gift to a minor, if over a small amount will require a court appointed guardian to manage the money until the ward turns 18. A somewhat better approach is to leave it to the minor in a Uniform Transfers to Minors Act account. That way the property can be controlled and managed until age 21. The best way to control property for a minor beneficiary is with a trust. That way property can be managed past age 21, and an environment can be established where the beneficiary gradually assumes control by first serving as a co-trustee so that the beneficiary can learn not only the ways of the investment world, but also start to gain a long term perspective of what the inheritance can become. An inheritance is not pennies from Heaven that is meant to be immediately spent, but rather a gift of love for which the beneficiary has an obligation of good stewardship.

How do I protect my child's inheritance from divorce?

With about 50% of the marriages in the United States end-ing in divorce, this is a major concern. Usually an inheritance will not be split in a divorce. However, the fly in the ointment is that if the inherited funds get co-mingled with other assets all bets are off. In addition, the judge may chose to disregard this rule if he or she feels it is not equitable. Why take that chance? Leaving a ben-eficiary's inheritance in trust protects against divorce.

Can a beneficiary be the trustee of their own trust share?

If the trust limits distributions to the ascertainable standard of health, education, maintenance and support, a beneficiary may serve as trustee and not have the trust assets included in their estate. This is reasonably broad discretion because maintenance means anything needed to maintain the beneficiary's lifestyle. However, for protection from lawsuits and bankruptcy the answer may be different. Basically, the greater the threat, the less control the beneficiary should have. Co-trustee provides more protection than being a sole trustee, but for maximum protection an inde-pendent trustee should be used.

What is a dynasty trust?

Good estate planning does not just solve a problem by push-ing it down to the next generation, but solves it for future gener-ations. A dynasty trust is designed to keep property outside of the estate tax system for future generations. There are limits on how much a person can pass this way, but a good rule is to take advan-tage of this limit to remove as much of your property as possible from the estate tax system because who knows what Congress will do in the future. It is better to write your own estate tax by using a dynasty trust. Besides, your tax system will have a better rate than the one designed by Congress.

While Congress determines the amount that can be left to future generations, how long it can be left is a matter of State Law. The issue is something called the Rule Against Perpetuities. This rule originated in the English Common Law and limited the length of time a trust could exist to the lifetime of someone who had already been born plus 21 years. The current trend is to eliminate this rule, and many states allow trusts to last forever.

A dynasty trust will create a separate trust for each beneficiary. Each beneficiary can then modify the dynasty trust before it is split into shares for the next generation of beneficiaries. This process then continues generation after generation. Because this trust is estate tax exempt, it will be worth far more than a trust that is taxed at each generation.

> *Win & Rosemarie's revocable trust evolved over the years. After a number of attorneys, and multiple restatements, they decided that their wishes were best met by providing for their family with a dynasty trust. With a dynasty trust their assets are protected for multiple future generations of the family, while allowing each beneficiary to control his or her trust share regarding investments, distributions and the final disposition.*

After my death can a beneficiary change how their trust share passes to the next generation?

Yes, this type of re-write power is called a power of appointment. Even thought the beneficiary is not the legal owner of the trust property, the power of appointment lets the beneficiary change the future beneficiaries and the terms of the trust shares.

Typically the beneficiary is authorized to exercise the power of appointment in either their will or living trust.

I want my cottage to stay in the family for future generations. How do I do that?

As time passes and the generations go from siblings to cousins and 2nd or 3rd cousins this becomes more and more difficult. The cottage needs to be left in an entity that can accommodate beneficiaries cashing out. A trust does not fit this structure. A Limited Liability Company (LLC) on the other hand is designed to have changing membership. The LLC allows the members to change the rules and to elect managers to maintain the property. It can provide the terms that allow the child who moves to California to sell his or her interest either to other members or back to the LLC.

It is not enough to just pass on the cottage. You also need to endow the cottage with enough funds to pay taxes, insurance, maintenance and utilities. Each of the beneficiaries will have a differing ability to pay for the upkeep. A certain way to start a family feud is to have to pass the hat each time something needs to be done to the cottage. An endowment for the cottage is the only way to make certain that all members of the family, regardless of wealth, get to use it.

How do I provide for personal property?

It is important for you to decide where your personal property goes. Although the personal property often is not valuable in monetary terms, it carries great stories that make it the most valuable inheritance from a sentimental viewpoint. If there is going to be a family fight it will most likely be over the dishes and Hummel's, not the stocks and bonds. Find out what your beneficiaries want, and document your decisions. One way is to list the personal property in your will or living trust. The disadvantage of this approach is that this type of gift frequently changes, and even if you get back to the lawyer each time there is a change this can get to be expensive. A better approach is to provide in your will or living trust that you will use personal property memos to distribute these items. This way you can make frequent changes and keep it affordable.

What about my funeral arrangements?

The time of your death will be very stressful for your loved ones. One of the most loving gifts you can make is to pre-plan your final arrangements. This includes the decision on cremation versus burial and the details of any funeral or memorial service you desire. The more details in your plan, the greater the load off of your loved ones shoulders. It is especially helpful to write a draft of your obituary. This is an item many families struggle with when they should be joining together to celebrate your life. As a final note, the best of plans isn't of any use if it can't be found. Include your instructions with the binder containing all of your estate planning documents, and make certain your family knows where to find them.

After my death, does anything need to be done if I have a trust?

Just because you don't have to go through probate doesn't mean nothing needs to be done. Taxes need to be filed, expenses and debts need to be paid, and titles need to be changed on assets. The list can be quite long. This process is called trust settlement and involves about as many steps as a probate. The difference is that the family is in charge, and not the judge. Therefore, your loved ones decide on the timeframe and who will do what. This is the reason a trust settlement is easier and less expensive. While probate costs may average about 3% to 5% of the estate assets, a trust settlement should cost only about a third as much.

How do I leave money to charities?

One of the best ways is to give to the charity during your lifetime. That way you get an income tax deduction plus the satisfaction of seeing the results of your generosity. At death you can leave money either as a specific distribution, which is a specific asset or dollar amount, or as a percentage of the estate. Assets left to charity are subtracted from the value of your estate for the purposes of calculating estate taxes. Families that are not going to have a taxable estate often leave the money to their beneficiaries with non-binding wishes that certain amounts be given to charity. This way the gift comes from the beneficiaries and therefore is a deduction from their income tax.

Nothing says that you have to leave the gift to a specific charity. An increasing trend is to leave the charitable portion of the estate to a family fund established at the local community foundation. The income from your gift can then be used for years to come and your beneficiaries can even be the fund advisors for the purpose of making suggestions about how to distribute the gift.

What is a charitable remainder trust?

A Charitable Remainder Trust (CRT) is a way of getting a current income tax deduction for a gift that is going to charity at your death, while retaining income from the donated asset. This is an irrevocable trust that will distribute its assets to charity when the trust terminates, usually at your death. The trust property will be included in your estate when you die, but the estate will receive an offsetting charitable deduction. You may serve as your own trustee and can retain the right to change charitable beneficiaries. The only thing that you are locked into is that the assets will go to charity on trust termination. At the time the trust is established you decide how much income, as a percentage, you are going to take out each year. This income, along with the current interest rate and your life expectancy determine the percentage of the donated assets that will be used as your income tax deduction.

Many people will transfer appreciated assets to a CRT so that they can be sold without any capital gains tax. The beneficiary can also be your family fund at the community foundation. That way the charities you supported during life can continue to receive gifts after your death. In summary, if you are certain you will be making charitable gifts at death, why not set up a CRT to get the income tax benefit?

What is a life insurance trust?

It is well known that life insurance proceeds received at death are tax free. What is not as well known is that this only means income tax free. The proceeds will be included in the value of your estate for the purpose of calculating estate taxes. If you have a taxable estate the insurance may only provide a benefit to your loved ones of about one half the face amount. The rest of the policy proceeds will go to the government in the form of estate taxes. This is especially painful because the reason many wealthy families have life insurance is to provide liquidity to the estate in order to pay the estate taxes.

An irrevocable life insurance trust, or ILIT, removes the insurance and proceeds from your estate. That way the full value of the policy will be available to loved ones. The process is fairly straight forward. The policy is either gifted or sold to the trustee of the ILIT, or in the case of a new policy the money for the premium payment is gifted to the ILIT. Each year additional funds are gifted to the ILIT. The trustee notifies the beneficiaries that a gift has been made and that they have a period of time to demand the gift. Once this period of time expires the gift can be used to pay the insurance premiums. Having described the process, it needs to be said that there are numerous ways to do this wrong. The good news is that you don't have to worry about small mistakes. The bad news is that any mistakes you make will be huge. Failing to do things exactly correctly could mean the inclusion of the policy in your estate and a very large, and unnecessary, tax bill. Only trust an ILIT to an attorney who is an expert in this area.

Although these trusts are called ILITs and are typically funded with insurance, nothing limits the type of asset you can transfer to an irrevocable gifting trust. The advantage of insurance is that there is no income tax on the cash buildup in the policy, and no tax on the proceeds. Insurance also gives a predictable result with the necessary cash available regardless of when you die. But, for someone who is not insurable, it is certainly possible to fund this type of trust with assets such as mutual funds, CDs or annuities.

> *Rosemarie and Win decided to set up an irrevocable life insurance trust (ILIT) to own their life insurance. With all of the uncertainty about death taxes, and the amount that can pass to their beneficiaries tax-free, it just didn't make sense to expose the insurance proceeds to possible taxes. The insurance was, after all, an investment they were making for their children's benefit, not their own.*

What if my whole family is wiped out?

It is important that your estate plan cover every possible contingency, even very remote ones. The likelihood of this possibility is a product of your family size and where everyone lives. The possible candidates to inherit your property in the event there are no immediate family members usually include your nearest living relatives or charities.

What is long term care?

In general the term long term care is used to describe the options for shelter and health care when you get to the point in your life where it is no longer possible to live on your own without some assistance. There are basically three options. The first is to remain in your own home with some type of in-home care. This can be a wonderful option if the needed level of care is limited in either scope or the number of hours. However, if skilled care is needed 24 hours a day this option is the most expensive and can cost almost twice what a nursing home charges. The advantage of in-home care is that you get to stay in the comfortable surroundings of your own home. The disadvantage is that the care is being provided in a location that was never designed with health care services in mind.

The second option, and the one that is growing at the fastest rate, is assisted living. The term assisted living can apply to a wide range of facilities. What most have in common is that you have your own apartment and your meals are provided in a community dining room. The level of care can vary from a low level that approximates independent living to a relatively high level of assistance. Of particular note are assisted living facilities that specialize is memory care (Alzheimer's). The more assistance provided, the higher the monthly cost. In general, for a moderate level of care, an assisted living facility will cost about half what a skilled nursing facility costs.

The last option is a nursing home. This option is generally the most expensive and the most restrictive form of custodial care. Here, instead of an apartment, most of the residents live in semi-private rooms. Because this is the only option that is covered by the government's Medicaid program, many individuals who lack sufficient financial resources are forced to move to a nursing home even though they could be adequately cared for in an assisted living facility or at home.

What are the chances I'll need long term care?

Studies have determined that up to 7 out of 10 people over the age of 65 will need some form of long term care. As discussed earlier, long term care comes in many forms. The fact that most people will need some form of care during their lifetimes illustrates the need to plan for such events.

How much does a nursing home cost?

The cost of nursing home care varies greatly between geographic regions and depends to a large extent on the type of care required. The costs associated with Alzheimer patients, for example, are likely to be much higher than the costs incurred by the patient with circulatory problems. A good estimate for the year 2010 would place the average cost somewhere between $6500 and $8000 per month, and like all health care related costs, the costs are climbing fast. The historic rate of increase in long term care costs has been 5% compounded. That means that by the year 2014 the cost of long term care will have doubled.

If I go to a nursing home, how will I pay for it?

There are three basic choices. First, pay for it yourself. This is the least complicated way and the easiest to implement, but the most painful when you are paying out major dollars to the nursing home that you would rather conserve for your spouse and family. Many people cannot stomach the idea that what they worked so hard to accumulate all of their life is now going to the nursing home.

The second funding choice is to divest your assets and qualify for Medicaid. This is often not easy to do and requires giving up control. It also takes away all options except for the nursing home. There is no guarantee, given the current government budget deficits, that this option will be available in the future.

The final and best option is to get a long term care insurance policy. This takes all of the uncertainty out of paying for long term care and preserves options such as home health care and assisted living, instead of limiting you to the nursing home. Long term care insurance is not inexpensive, but you should strongly consider it because it keeps you in control. The sooner you start planning the better the chances that this option will be available to you.

Will Medicare pay for my long term care?

Medicare will not pay for custodial care in the nursing home, but it will pay for rehabilitative care in a nursing home setting for a limited time. Typically, Medicare will pay for the first 20 days in the nursing home for those patients receiving physical therapy or other rehabilitative treatment. To qualify for Medicare coverage, a patient's nursing home stay must have been preceded by a three-day, or longer, hospital stay.   Medicare will then pay a portion of the next 80 days in a nursing home. After 100 days, Medicare will, in virtually all cases, cease payment. Medicare does have the ability to terminate coverage before the 100-day period elapses if the patient is not making progress towards rehabilitation and recovery.

What is long term care insurance?

Long term care insurance is an insurance product designed to pay some or all of a policy holder's long term care needs. As discussed earlier, long term care comes in several forms; home health care, assisted living, and nursing homes are a few of the most recognized forms. It is strongly recommended that anybody with a concern about potential nursing home costs consult with a qualified long term care insurance professional about a policy. This should be your first approach to addressing your concern. Furthermore, recently enacted Federal Legislation has given individual states the authority to implement extraordinarily beneficial "partnership" programs that may provide dramatic additional incentives to long term care insurance holders. Each state will address this opportunity differently, so it is imperative that you consult with a knowledgeable insurance professional in your state.

Long term care insurance is expensive, isn't it?

Not necessarily. Certainly there are people with existing health concerns that would find, because of their condition, that even the most basic long term care policy would be prohibitively expensive. Also, if you get a quote on the Cadillac of long term care policies with all the bells and whistles built in, you might find that such a policy can be rather pricey. However, if you work with a competent, trusted insurance professional and design a long term policy specifically for your needs, goals, and budget, you will likely find that, as long as you can qualify for the policy from a medical standpoint, you will be able to afford it with relative ease. Keep in mind that the monthly cost of staying in a nursing home is typically larger than the annual cost of the long term care premium. Once you realize the size of the risk that you are insuring against, the cost of the premium may seem less expensive.

A common mistake that people make is assuming that, because they have a medical condition, they cannot get long term care insurance. While it is true that some medical conditions will disqualify you for coverage, you cannot know for sure without working with a qualified long term care insurance professional. Many policies exist that will cover certain conditions, and the industry is constantly developing and evolving. You have to consult a professional before you can make a truly educated decision.

Win and Rosemarie decided, after analyzing the potentially devastating cost of long term care, to take out long term care insurance policies. Even though they are not inexpensive, the policies gave them the peace of mind and the greatest flexibility for whatever care needs they might face in the future. Their only regret is that they did not get policies with a cost of living adjustment feature.

Should I give my assets to my children?

The key to proper estate planning is to keep as much control of your life and your assets as possible. Giving your assets to your children does not allow you much control. Now, not only are the assets out of your control, but they are also subject to all of your children's creditors, the stability of their marriages, and their financial difficulties. Good long term care planning protects your assets, while giving assets to the children subjects them to additional risk. Assets should only be divested as part of a carefully crafted plan developed with the assistance of a qualified professional advisor. A carefully designed custom plan will allow you to keep the greatest degree of control for the longest period of time.

Will the Nursing home take my House?

Typically, for purposes of determining qualification, the Medicaid office will ignore the personal residence of a Medicaid applicant. This is especially true for married couples. You could be living in a house costing $500,000 or more and still qualify for Medicaid as long as the other criteria are met.

Always talk to a qualified estate and Medicaid planning attorney prior to transferring the residence. The transfer of the house may be a viable and important transaction, but it is often just a matter of timing. Do it at the wrong time or under the wrong circumstances and you will be creating more problems than you are solving.

Will my Revocable Living Trust protect my assets from nursing home costs?

A revocable trust is an important part of any estate plan that is designed to protect your family's assets from nursing home costs, but by itself a revocable trust will not protect your assets. Trusts are the preferred way to protect assets, but the types of trusts that are used for this purpose are irrevocable trusts that hold assets you have given away. Because irrevocable trusts remove assets from your direct control it is not generally recommended that you transfer your assets to them until it is a near certainty you will need this type of planning. Therefore, the preferred way to plan is to set up a revocable trust along with powers of attorney that provide for someone being designated to implement your nursing home plan on your behalf, if you are unable to do so yourself.

How do I qualify for Medicaid?

To qualify for Medicaid, a person must meet two primary economic criteria. The first criterion is income; a resident in a nursing home that is seeking to qualify for Medicaid must have income that is less than the cost of care. The Medicaid resident is allowed to keep a small amount of their monthly income for personal needs. Typically this amount is less than $100; the balance of the monthly income is paid to the nursing home for cost of care. Medicaid will then pay the balance.

For nursing home patients with spouses living at home, income is handled differently. In many states, the spouse at home is not required to contribute any of his or her own income to the cost of care for the nursing home spouse. If the spouse at home has little or no income, he or she can pull some income from the nursing home spouse to supplement their own income.

The second economic criterion is assets. A person residing in a nursing home must spend down their cash assets to a very low level. The spend-down target can be as low as $2000. For married couples, the calculation is more complex. The spouse that remains in the home is allowed to keep a larger percentage of the family's cash assets. There are certain assets that the Medicaid office does not count when determining the target asset level. These non-countable assets may include the family home, the family car, personal belongings, burial assets, and a small amount of life insurance. See your estate and Medicaid planning attorney for a review and complete explanation of these complex rules.

Do I get to choose my nursing home?

Your options for choosing a nursing home are best if you enter as a "private pay." This means you are initially paying with your own assets or with long term care insurance. If you enter the nursing home on Medicaid you may have more limited options. Most nursing homes will have a limited number of "Medicaid beds." If there are no Medicaid beds available locally you might wind up in a nursing home that is not in your community, and will be very difficult for your loved ones to get to for frequent visits. Therefore, the best option is to enter as "private pay" so that you preserve your choices. This is one of the reasons people get long term care insurance, even if the policy benefit is for a limited period of time.

Can the nursing home kick me out if I run out of money?

If the nursing home takes Medicaid reimbursement they can not kick you out. This is true even if they do not have a "Medicaid bed" available. Only a small number of nursing homes don't take Medicaid, so in most cases you will be able to stay in the same semi-private room you had when you were paying with your own money. If you were in a private room they will be able to move you to a semi-private room when you go on Medicaid, unless your family is able to pay the difference in cost, but you won't be out on the street. Because it is possible that the nursing home you select doesn't take Medicaid reimbursement, it is always a good idea to check this out before you enter if there is any chance you will run out of money to pay for the nursing home.

I'm on a fixed income; how will I make ends meet if my spouse goes to the nursing home?

It is not the government's intent to impoverish the spouse who remains at home. In general, the "community spouse" gets to keep all of his or her income. In addition, if the community spouse has a low level of income he or she will get some or all of the "nursing home" spouse's income. This minimum amount of income varies from state to state, but in most areas is about $2,500 per month. As an example, assume the husband is in the nursing home and the wife (community spouse) is allowed $2,500. If her only income is $600 of social security, she would be eligible to take up to $1,900 of the husband's income. If the husband in the nursing home has less than $1,400 of income the wife would get it all. In other words, if the couple has less than $2,500 in income the community spouse keeps it all, but the government does not make any payments to the community spouse for the amount under $2,500.

My child lives with me, what happens if I go to the nursing home?

It is a fairly common situation for a child to live in your house and provide assistance that allows you to remain at home. It would be sad indeed if after this sacrifice your child was thrown out of the house after you went into the nursing home. Fortunately, this is unlikely to happen. As long as a child lives in your house for at least two years prior to your going into the nursing home, and they helped you stay in your home, then they will be able to remain in the house. With appropriate proof the home can be transferred to the child without incurring a divestment penalty.

I am single. Is there a limit to the assets that I can own and still qualify for Medicaid?

As a single person you must "spend down" your assets to a very low level before you are qualified to receive Medicaid assistance for your nursing home bills. The amount you are allowed to keep varies from state to state, with $2,000 being the most common limit. Not counted in this limit are certain exempt assets such as a modestly priced car, a small amount of life insurance, personal property and funds designated for your burial. Your personal residence will not be counted in the asset limit if you have expressed an intent to return to your home. However, the government may place a lien on your home that will be paid when the house is sold.

If my spouse goes to the nursing home, will I have to spend all of our money?

No. Your State has a set of rules designed to ensure that having one spouse residing in a nursing home will not have the effect of completely devastating the other spouse's finances as well. These rules are commonly referred to as the Spousal Impoverishment rules. Typically, the spouse at home is allowed to retain one-half of the cash assets that the couple had on the day the other spouse went into the nursing home. There are however minimum and maximums to consider. The maximum amount most states will allow the community spouse to retain is in the neighborhood of $110,000. This amount will typically be adjusted on a yearly basis to take into account inflation. The minimum spend-down target varies from state to state, but $50,000 is a good average.

To get to the spend-down target, there is really only one rule: the community spouse must get value in return for the money spent. If the assets are given away, the state will view that transfer as a "divestment," and such uncompensated transfers will be penalized. The "spend down" process is where the creativeness, resourcefulness, and knowledge of your planning team will truly pay dividends. Spending down without incurring excessive periods of ineligibility while, at the same time, ensuring the assets are being used effectively and in a manner that the assets are protected is the most important goal in planning.

If I give away assets, do I have to wait 5 years until I go into the nursing home?

In general, when you make a gift it will cause you to be disqualified from receiving Medicaid for a period of time. The number of days of ineligibility is calculated by dividing the amount of the gift by the amount that Medicaid will pay for a day of nursing home care. The beginning of the penalty period coincides with the date on which you are residing in a nursing home and, except for the gift, are otherwise qualified to file a Medicaid application.

What about annuities?

The basic idea behind using annuities in the Medicaid area is to convert what otherwise would be considered an at-risk cash asset of the nursing home spouse to an income stream of the community spouse which will be protected from the "spend down" process. Annuities may also be used as a means to "buy" your way through a penalty period imposed on transfers that you have made. Like any tool, when used in the proper circumstances they can be indispensable asset protection techniques.

What is "divestment?"

Divestment, simply put, is a transfer of an asset where you do not get full value in return for the asset transferred. Giving money or other assets to your kids will be considered a divestment. People often ask about the $13,000 per year that you are allowed to transfer. That $13,000 is an annual exclusion amount that refers to gift tax issues, and has no bearing on the Medicaid rules. Similarly, transferring assets to a charity may also be considered a divestment. Forgiving a debt is yet another form of divestment that will get some people in trouble. During the Medicaid application review process every divestment that appears on your financial records will be assessed a penalty.

If I am disabled, can somebody make gifts on my behalf?

This is a very important question. If you do become disabled and have no base level planning in place, it is likely that it will be left to a judge to appoint a guardian to make your decisions for you. In situations such as this, the court-appointed guardian has little or no ability to plan for your long term care needs if such planning involves a divestment plan.

It is vitally important that you have a comprehensive estate plan in place that will preserve the ability for your chosen helpers to prepare a long term care plan, including a divestment plan, for you if you were to become disabled. Being able to "cross that bridge when you come to it" through comprehensive estate planning ensures that you leave your options open and maintain control of your assets as long as possible.

Are the rules for VA benefits the same as for Medicaid?

No they are not. These are separate programs that have different qualification criteria and different rules concerning asset levels and divestment. In addition, VA benefits are limited to veterans who have served during a period of war. The benefits are, in general, either compensation, which is payment for disability tied to military service, or pension payments which are available to veterans, and to spouses of deceased veterans, who qualify based upon either low levels of income or high medical expenses.

How do I know if I qualify for VA benefits?

In general the Veterans Administration has done a very poor job of informing veterans about possible pension benefits. The best plan is to seek the assistance of someone who has been accredited by the VA as a benefits advisor. In order to give advice concerning veteran's benefits the VA requires advisors be accredited. There are a few accredited claims agents, but most of the VA accredited advisors are attorneys. Be careful, because not all attorneys who do Medicaid planning are accredited by the VA.

What are the types of VA pension benefits?

If the veteran, or the surviving spouse of a veteran, qualifies they can receive either a basic pension, a higher pension for being homebound, or a pension called Aid and Attendance if they are in need of medical assistance. The Aid and Attendance benefit is especially helpful because, unlike Medicaid, it will help defray long term care costs if the recipient is either receiving care at home or is in assisting living.

What are the asset limits for VA qualification?

Although the VA states an upper limit of $80,000 in assets, in practice the limit usually is lower. The VA's position is that you should be required to use some of your assets for your care. Therefore, the amount you can have depends upon your marital status and life expectancy. A married veteran will normally be allowed to keep more assets than a single veteran or a surviving spouse. For a single person, the limit appears to be no more than $50,000 in assets. In addition, a younger veteran with a longer life expectancy is usually allowed a higher level of assets than an older veteran. The justification is that the older veteran doesn't have as many years left to pay for needed care, and therefore needs fewer assets.

What if I have too many assets to qualify for a VA pension?

Just as with Medicaid qualification, you will need to divest the excess assets. The good news is that, unlike Medicaid, the VA does not penalize you for the divestment. So, instead of waiting up to five years, as with Medicaid qualification, you can be qualified immediately after the divestment for a VA pension.

The other difference from Medicaid is that the VA does not allow you to retain a life estate in any real estate other than your personal residence, and does not allow you to put assets into a trust from which you receive income. Basically, if you get income from it, the asset counts as being owned by you for the purpose of determining benefit qualification.

Did the veteran need to serve in combat to qualify?

No, the only requirement is that the veteran served at least one day during time of war, as part of a minimum 90 day deployment that was for other than training purposes. The critical dates are:

- World War II – 12/7/1941 to 7/25/1947

- Korean conflict – 6/27/1950 to 12/31/1955

- Vietnam War – 8/5/1964 to 5/7/1975

Do I need to be disabled to qualify for VA pension benefits?

Yes, you do. However, the VA considers anyone over the age of 65 as disabled. Thus, any WWII or Korean era veteran will be considered disabled, and many of the older Vietnam veterans will also qualify.

My ex-spouse was a wartime veteran. Do I qualify as a surviving spouse?

In order to qualify as a surviving spouse, you must have been married to the deceased veteran at least a year and also been married on the date of his or her death. In other words, if you were divorced, you do not qualify. In addition, if you were married to a wartime veteran at the time of his or her death, but later remarried, you would only be qualified if the new spouse was a veteran.

What is the amount of the VA pension?

The amount of the pension will adjust for inflation, but at the time of this writing, the basic pension for a veteran is about $1,000 per month. If the veteran is homebound the amount goes up to about $1,200 per month. Finally, if the veteran qualifies for the Aid and Attendance benefit the pension is over $1600 per month. The pension amount for a surviving spouse is approximately two-thirds of the veteran's pension. If the veteran is married, the pension amount increases by just over $300 per month. These are maximum amounts, and the actual pension will depend on the level of income. Regardless of the amount, VA pensions are not taxable.

How is the actual pension amount calculated?

The first step is to calculate your income for VA pension purposes (IVAP). The IVAP is your gross income minus certain deductions. Almost all of these deductions are for un-reimbursed medical costs. This is a long list, but the most important ones are your Medicare supplement premium, medications and any deductibles and co-pays you actually paid. These deductions reduce your gross income to IVAP. The IVAP is now compared to the maximum pension amount for which you qualify. Thus, if the IVAP is more than the pension, you get nothing. If it is less, you get the difference, and if the IVAP is zero or negative, you qualify for the maximum pension. In most cases you will get little or no pension benefit unless you have high un-reimbursed medical expenses. If you need home health care, or need to be in an assisted living facility, all of these costs are considered medical expenses. Therefore, the major impact of a VA pension is that it may allow the veteran or surviving spouse to avoid going into a nursing home (which is the only long term care option paid by Medicaid) by providing extra income for care at home or in assisted living.

CHAPTER SEVEN

CHARITABLE GIVING

Gary Roth, Maria Kees & Kim Petersen

Previous chapters discussed wise stewardship of money. This chapter deals with the opportunities and strategies available when we charitably give from our resources. Whether savings have come from the use of sound financial principles or from inherited wealth, there is tremendous satisfaction in giving to charitable causes.

Various reasons motivate people to be charitably inclined. Several give to religious organizations as a result of their beliefs and values. Many people donate out of the desire to give back to their communities or to organizations that have helped them in the past. Other individuals give as a result of their fondness for a specific cause. Some give to charity to pass on values or to create legacies that will last into the future. Many strive to pass on to their children not only assets, but more importantly, values such as generosity, integrity, and social responsibility through wise stewardship of assets.

A person can make a difference in several ways; waiting until finances are in good order is not always necessary. Donating a specified percentage of income is one way to regularly contribute to a good cause. This way, as your income increases, so does your charitable contribution. In addition, many needs can be filled without giving money but rather by volunteering time and talent. Examples include serving at a local food pantry, helping with community projects that address homelessness or poverty, and assisting with youth programs at local schools, churches, or mentoring organizations.

Charitable Planning

For those who have the means and desire to donate, a written charitable plan serves as a highly effective way to define goals, determine how to make the best use of charitable dollars, and decide how to leave a lasting legacy. When preparing and setting up a charitable plan, the help of professionals is essential. Potential resources include an estate planning attorney, financial planner, tax advisor, and personnel from a local community foundation or your favorite charitable organizations. These professionals will help design and facilitate strategies used to accomplish charitable goals.

A charitable plan gives concrete direction to a charitable philosophy. The charitable intent can be clarified in a plan by determining the:

- Charities to support
- Methods to maximize benefit to the charities
- Strategies to reduce or eliminate federal income and estate taxes
- Best time to donate

Evaluating Charities

When giving to charity, the donor may not have the ability to control how the funds are used. Nevertheless, research can be done on an organization prior to donating to understand how the charity operates.

Charities can be researched by requesting brochures or financial statements, and by doing research online. Agencies are set up to provide information on and ratings of charitable organizations and can give donators an idea of how donations are allocated. This information can include what percentage of donations are typically allocated to the cause and what is spent on overhead, including salaries, administrative costs, and marketing, among other things. Informative agencies include Better Business Bureau's Wise Giving Alliance, Charity Navigator, Guidestar, and the American Institute of Philanthropy. If there are questions left unanswered, talk with the organization's leaders.

Maximize Your Donation

Look for opportunities to increase the effect of your donations. For example, there are many opportunities to double donation dollars through matching programs. Several employers are willing to match gifts made by employees to qualified charities. In addition, public television auctions and telethons announce times during which contributions will be matched by another donor.

Organizations in the Fox Valley area offer programs to match contributions and keep them local. For instance, on certain days throughout the year, donations to The Salvation Army are matched by local companies. Another matching opportunity is available through the U.S. Venture Open Fund for Basic Needs. This fund, through the Community Foundation for the Fox Valley

Region, raises millions of dollars each year to help fight the root causes of poverty throughout Northeast Wisconsin. From the total funds raised by the annual U.S. Venture Open, 10% is distributed each year throughout local communities. This 10% distribution is matched by the JJ Keller Foundation, thereby maximizing contributions to this fund.

Contact U.S. Venture Open Fund for Basic Needs at:

425 Better Way
Appleton, WI 54915
920-739-6101

Tax Benefits

Tax benefits offer another opportunity to maximize donations. Many people enjoy the gratification that comes with charitable giving for the purpose of helping others. In addition to the joy of donating, there are tax advantages in providing financial resources to tax-qualified charities. These tax-qualified charitable organizations are often referred to as 501(c)(3) organizations. The government encourages and rewards charitable giving, and as a result, contributions to these organizations are tax-deductible, up to certain limits.

Cash is the most common asset contributed to charity. A gift of cash is usually as simple as writing out a check payable to your favorite organization. Many charities also accept credit card gifts online or over the phone, and an increasing number of organizations are able to set up automatic monthly contributions from your bank account. Some employers also allow contributions to be made through payroll deductions. Ask the staff or leaders of your favorite charities about the different options available, so that you can choose the one most convenient for you and the organization.

Another common gift is appreciated securities – that is, publicly traded stocks, bonds, or mutual fund shares that have increased in value since you acquired them. If you have owned the securities for at least 12 months, you will enjoy a double tax benefit: in addition to a charitable income tax deduction for the value of the securities on the date you give them, you will also avoid capital gains tax on the appreciation. Most charities are able to accept gifts of securities; if your favorite cause does not have the systems in place to do so, consult your local community foundation, which may be able to facilitate the gift for you.

Each charitable strategy or organization has its own purpose and comes with its own set of regulations. Setting the strategies up properly requires an understanding that typically only comes with the help of a professional. For instance, if a sizable gift is being contemplated, there are regulation limits to eligible tax deductions. Charitable cash contributions are eligible for up to 50% of the adjusted gross income. For contributions of appreciated securities or property, 30% of the adjusted gross income is allowed. Amounts exceeding the limit may be able to be carried forward and deducted over the next five years.

When to Make Charitable Donations

From the tax planning point of view, it is typically more beneficial to make charitable gifts while living rather than upon death because income tax deductions are received during the lifetime that may not be obtained with gifts made after death. In addition, lifetime gifts allow the donor to further leverage philanthropy upon death because of income tax deductions received while living. This situation occurs because assets are moved out of the donor's estate and will no longer be subject to estate taxes.

Beyond the tax benefits, there are various reasons to donate to charitable causes while living:

- Set an example to heirs
- Enjoy personal satisfaction of making the gift – know that your assets went to help a cause that is meaningful to you
- Monitor and see the results of the charity's use of the gift

Many of us make our most sizeable gifts at death, after our own personal, family, and financial matters have been settled. These gifts need not be complicated, and can be as simple or easy as naming favorite charities as a beneficiary on retirement accounts or insurance policies. Somewhat more involved are gifts made under your will or through a trust; an attorney's assistance is needed to prepare the documents. Because the value of your assets will change over time, it is usually a good idea to provide for a percentage of your estate, rather than a fixed dollar amount, to go to your favorite charities. Measuring the charitable portion of your estate in percentage terms means that your gifts to family, friends, and loved ones will stay in balance with your gifts to charity, regardless whether your assets grow or fall in value from year to year.

Some gift plans allow you to support your favorite causes at death while providing you or a loved one with income for life. The most common such gift is a charitable gift annuity. With a charitable gift annuity, the donor gives a gift to the charity and the charity agrees to pay an annual payment to the beneficiary for the remainder of the beneficiary's life. Upon the beneficiary's death, the agreement terminates and the charity is under no further obligation. The remaining amount that has not been distributed as income to the beneficiary is the amount allocated to charity.

The donor is entitled to a charitable deduction in the year of the original gift. This deduction is calculated by determining the present value of the annuity payments and subtracting that value from the gift amount. During the beneficiary's IRS-determined life expectancy, the beneficiary receives some of the annuity as tax-free income and the rest is ordinary income. The interest rate given by the charity is a fixed rate based on the age of the beneficiary to the annuity. The older the beneficiary is, the higher the rate.

Charitable Strategies

Many may believe they don't have enough to start a significant giving plan, but it does not take a great deal of wealth for someone to get started contributing to charity. Modest donations are welcome, and often essential, for many organizations.

Community Foundation

A community foundation is a tax-exempt, public charity established by many separate donors. The intent is to support charitable organizations in a particular geographical region with the goal of improving the quality of life of its residents. Gifts to community foundations can be endowed, which means income is generated from the gift and will be distributed to the charitable beneficiaries each year into the future. Locate your nearest community foundation through the "Community Foundation Locator" at www.cof.org.

Contact the local community foundation in Wisconsin's Fox Valley at:

Community Foundation for the Fox Valley Region
PO Box 563 – 4455 W. Lawrence Street
Appleton, WI 54912-0563
(920) 830-1290
http://www.cffoxvalley.org

Community foundations generally maintain several funds, each serving a specific charitable purpose. Some funds are supported by many donors. Other funds are targeted to a particular donor's interests and usually require a minimum contribution amount. Funds include:

Unrestricted Fund

Unrestricted donations can be made to the community foundation, and each year, the foundation's professional staff will decide how to best allocate the funds throughout various areas of the community. These donations can be extremely beneficial because as a community's needs change, the fund allocations can be adjusted to fit the ever-changing needs of the community. Tax benefits are received in the year the gift is made. Gifts may be made during the donor's lifetime or upon death.

Donor Advised Funds

Donor advised funds are charitable giving programs generally administered by third party public charities that allow the maximum income tax deduction at the time of the gift. The charity administering the fund, such as a community foundation, has control over contributions, but the donor is typically granted donor advisory status. While not legally bound to the donor, grants to other qualified public charities are usually made at the donor's recommendation.

Upon counseling with their financial advisor, attorney, and tax advisor, Win and Rosemarie set up a donor advised fund at the Community Foundation for the Fox Valley Region. They have used the fund to make charitable contributions to their favorite causes, including a gift to the U.S. Venture Open Fund for Basic Needs.

Designated Funds

In a designated fund, the donor chooses one or more specific charitable organizations to benefit from the gift. Through the community foundation, the gifted funds are professionally managed and distributed to the organization on a regular basis. Tax benefits are received in the year the gift is made.

Field of Interest Funds

Field of interest funds are set up to benefit a specific cause. The donor may start a new fund to address a specific area of concern or designate the gift to an existing fund. Examples of field of interest funds include funds set up to benefit environmental issues, the arts, health care, and human services.

Scholarship Funds

Scholarship funds allow a donor to support students graduating from a particular high school, attending a certain college, or pursuing a specific course of study.

Private Foundation

A private foundation is a tax-exempt organization typically created by one individual, family or entity for the purpose of ongoing charitable giving. Currently, the largest private foundation in the U. S. is the Bill & Melinda Gates Foundation, with over $30 billion in assets.

Whatever the intent is for giving, the desire to share our blessings is evident. As a nation, Americans are a giving people; no other country gives as much. In recent years, Americans have annually provided over $300 billion to charitable causes. While we hear about the extremely wealthy giving large, generous donations, it doesn't take enormous wealth to make a difference. Modest-sized donations often provide the majority of charitable funds to organizations seeking such donations.

The satisfaction in giving is in becoming part of the solution to a problem. Including charitable giving in your financial plan is rewarding to both you and to those served by charitable gifts. For more information on charitable planning or to begin your charitable strategy, contact your financial advisor or a local community foundation.

EPILOGUE

Financial literacy education is essential for people from all walks of life; poor or rich, young or seniors, and everyone in-between. Practical knowledge of financial matters is always important, but especially critical in this world of economic turmoil and high unemployment. As healthy roots nurture the life force of a tree, so will a solid foundation in financial literacy nurture your personal and financial growth.

In Part One, Maung Win shared his personal experiences and lessons learned in the humble hope that the reader might gain insight and inspiration for dealing with his or her own potential difficulties.

Part Two began by addressing basic financial literacy education and moved on to sophisticated financial and life planning strategies. The Wealth Management Process© diagram on page 156 summarizes the financial literacy education dialogue that has been covered in the book.

The individual process segments delineated on the diagram are interrelated. As illustrated, the wealth management process begins at the top of the diagram and moves clockwise, highlighting the importance of spending less to save more. This concept, which is a cornerstone to effective financial planning, was covered in-depth in Chapter 1, Fundamentals of Financial Planning.

One needs to be an informed and educated investor to invest prudently and to manage accumulated assets via appropriate risk management techniques. To maximize investment success, an investor must understand investment strategies, concepts, and principles as well as proper diversification and asset allocation, risk management, tax implications and types of investment products. Due to the broad scope of knowledge and expertise required, a well-rounded approach to successful financial planning recommends seeking a financial planner who collaborates with a group of other key experts. (See Chapter 2, Investment Planning.)

In Chapter 3, Retirement Planning, balancing income and growth investments to preserve wealth were discussed. Investments which are too conservative may not beat or keep up with inflation, while investments which are too aggressive run the risk of losing principal in an economic downturn. You are cautioned to not depend on employer pension plans, but are encouraged to take advantage of employer-sponsored retirement plans and actively participate in IRAs.

As noted in Chapter 5, IRA Planning for Family Fortune, when IRAs are managed well and transferred to heirs efficiently, not only are tax advantages realized, but the fortune and legacy passed on to future generations is greatly enhanced. The final phase of the planning process is transferring wealth to heirs and/or charity. Examples of building wealth for retirement and passing on a legacy have been shared in Chapter 4, Insurance Planning, in Chapter 6 on Estate Planning and throughout the book. Philanthropy is discussed in Chapter 7, Charitable Giving.

The authors believe that people can achieve a better quality of life, prosperity, personal enrichment, family well-being and philanthropy through well-applied financial literacy education. We hope that this book has given you both the information and the inspiration to apply these concepts in your own life.

Finally, a promise Maung Win made during the darkest years of his life, and a dream of helping people by providing financial literacy education, have come to fruition.

©2006 M. H. Win &
K. Bidwell-Loberg

ABOUT THE AUTHORS

Maung Win, CFP® - has been a pro-bono financial educator with FISC since 1996. FISC (Financial Information and Service Center), a program of Goodwill Industries of North Central Wisconsin, is a non-profit 501(c) (3) that teaches the application of sound financial principles. M. Win's educational and planning services include money management, personal financial planning, investment principles and application, and retirement/post-retirement planning. His emphasis is on saving more for retirement by managing cash flow efficiently, and on educating individuals to become better informed investors.

Prior to becoming a financial planner, Win spent a total of 31 years with three S&P Fortune 100 companies as an engineer, technical leader and research and development manager. He was awarded eleven US patents in product and process development, and holds five copyrights in financial planning.

M. Win has a BS in Chemical Engineering, MS in Management and is a CFP® certificant. Maung has over 25 years of successful investment experience. He is a board member of FPA (Financial Planning Association), North East Wisconsin Chapter, and a member of SCORE, Small Business Counseling Group.

Edward F. (Foss) Hooper is the owner of Hooper Law office, a Wisconsin estate planning law firm with offices in Appleton and Green Bay, Wisconsin. His practice is concentrated in estate planning, Medicaid planning, veteran benefits planning, business succession planning, and probate and trust settlement services.

Foss received a Bachelor of Science degree in Economics and a Master of Science degree in Business Management from Rensselaer Polytechnic Institute in Troy, New York. After graduation, he served as a Captain in the United States Army and was a Senior Systems Engineer for IBM. Foss attended Marquette University Law School where he received his Juris Doctor degree summa cum laude. Attorney Hooper received the George L. Laikin Award in estate planning, the Joseph I. Swietlik Award in taxation, and the Law Alumni Award for having the highest academic average in his class.

Attorney Hooper is a founding member of the Wisconsin Council of Estate Planning Attorneys; a member of WealthCounsel; a member of ElderCounsel; and also earned the CExP (Certified Exit Planner) designation from the Business Enterprise Institute, a national organization dedicated to working with teams of advisors to develop comprehensive business exit plans.

Foss and his wife, Mary, live in Neenah, Wisconsin and Phoenix, Arizona. Their daughter, Beth, is married to Lawrence and works as an advertising executive in Chicago. Son, Ted, is a CPA and lives in Phoenix along with wife, Melissa and sons Edward and Wesley. In 2009, to celebrate his sixty-fifth birthday, Foss climbed Mount Kilimanjaro, the "roof" of Africa.

Robert S. Keebler, CPA, MST, AEP (Distinguished) is a partner with Keebler & Associates, LLP. He is a 2007 recipient of the prestigious Distinguished Estate Planners award from the National Association of Estate Planning Counsels. From 2003 to 2006, Mr. Keebler has been named by CPA Magazine as one of the top 100 most influential practitioners in the United States. His practice includes family wealth transfer and preservation planning, charitable giving, retirement distribution planning, and estate administration. Mr. Keebler frequently represents clients before the IRS National Office in the private letter ruling process and in estate, gift and income tax examinations and appeals, and he has received more than 150 favorable private letter rulings including several key rulings of "first impression." He is the author of over 100 articles and columns and is the editor, author, or co-author of many books and treatises on wealth transfer and taxation.

Kay Bidwell Loberg worked with FISC Consumer Credit Counseling Service as a Certified Consumer Credit Counselor, Financial Educator, and Assistant Agency Director. FISC, the Financial Information and Service Center, is a non-profit 501(c) (3) that teaches and encourages application of sound financial principles. Kay has written many articles on basic financial issues; produced a column, Speaking of Money, for a local newspaper; and has given presentations on a variety of financial topics to high school, community and workplace groups.

Currently, Kay is a free-lance writer, Board President of FISC of Sturgeon Bay, WI, and Office Manager with Advocates for Independent Living. She's a fiddler in the Cajun band, Envie, and plays with both a barn dance orchestra and Global Achord, an international folk group. Folk singer and songwriter, Kay enjoys dancing with her husband, Bruce.

Kay has two fiscally responsible sons, one an aspiring screen writer living in Washington state, and the other a college student living in Wisconsin.

Allen Win is the CEO of Flatline Design Inc., a graphic design studio specializing in web, digital and traditional design, illustration, animation and 3-D modeling.

He graduated from the School of Visual Arts in New York with a BFA in Illustration. Allen started his career working for an advertising agency, essentially being a one-man production and design department. He was able to leverage that experience with his knowledge of digital design and desktop publishing systems, to gain a position at Estée Lauder, Inc. There he was employed as a production artist for Prescriptives and Clinique, eventually becoming lead designer and team manager of their multimedia events. After working as a graphic artist in New York City for many years, Allen relocated to New Mexico. He has continued to maintain a strong relationship with Estée Lauder, and many of their brands are counted among his clientele.

Currently, he and his wife, Jude, live in Albuquerque, where they run Flatline Design, and are raising their two children, Alexander and Anique.

In his elusive free time, Allen studies and crafts Japanese swords, practices kenjutsu and karate, and researches Asian and World War II history.